Colorful
Portraits of Spring

book & photography by
Jodi Marie Fisher

all photographs taken in the Northwestern United States

Printed in the United States of America
First Edition 2019
Colorful Portraits of Spring

ISBN-13: 978-1071306413
ISBN-10: 1071306413

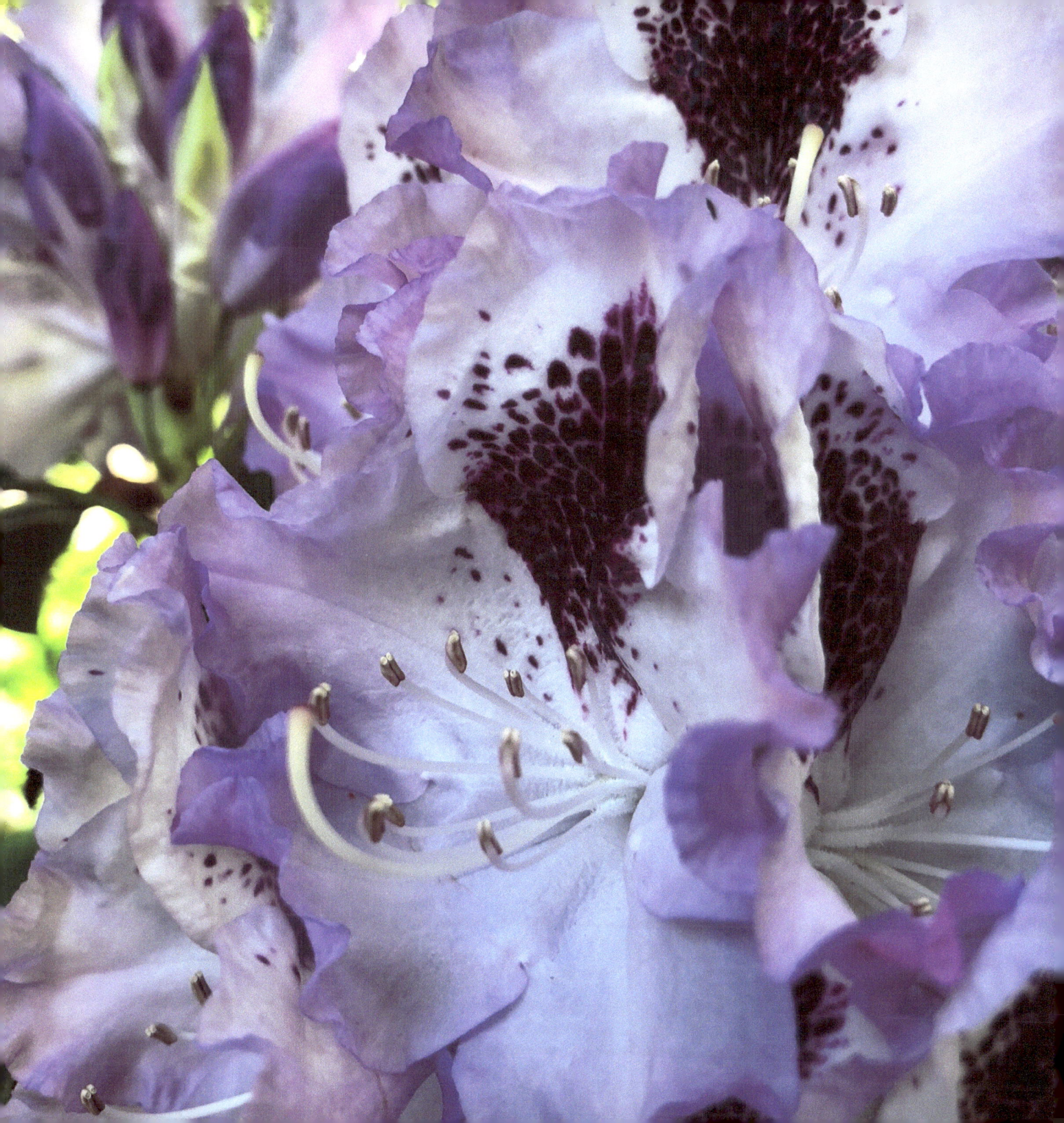

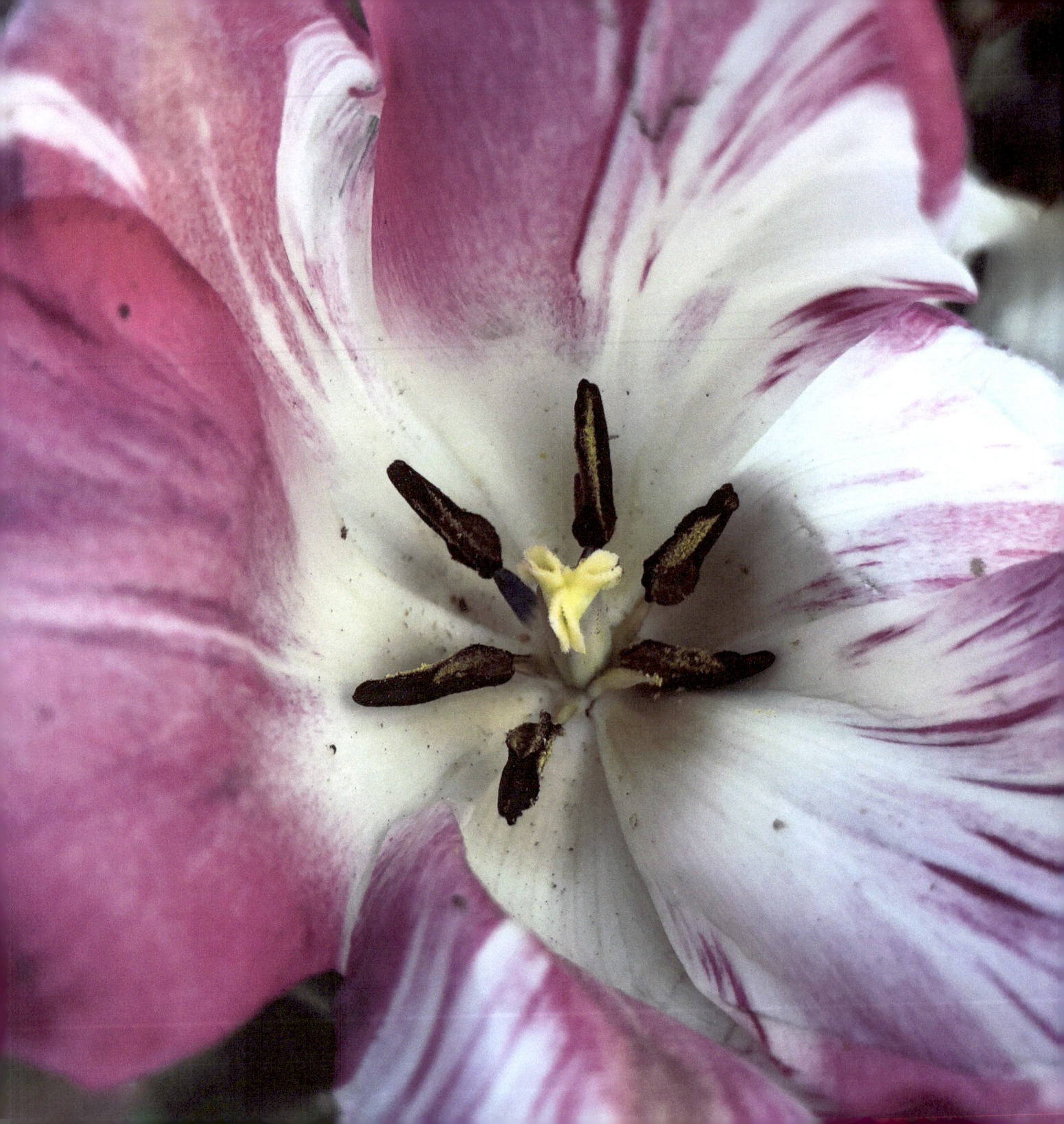

What are Colorful portraits of spring?

Seasons have portraits. **Faces. Personalities. Characteristics** you can recognize. When you see a familiar face. A family member. A friend. Even a stranger. Their portrait is distinct. Though some are similar and many almost the same, no one face is the same in people and the same is true in portraits of nature.

This book of colorful portraits of nature displays many, yet certainly not even close to all, of some of the faces you recognize in spring. Sping is most characterized by the rebirth of flowers and life around us after the cold and sometimes harsh winter. Spring gives new life and color to a blank canvas. Nature starts over again and so do we.

When you look out at a spring scene, all you may see is flowers, but if you look closely, you will see some incredibly beautiful faces inviting you to appreciate the season. Spring flowers alone, are as unique as snowflakes, and display an increidble variety of colors and characteristics. Each flower is unique in its own beauty.

Yet, it's easy to just see flowers as all the same. So, allow yourself to think about the little nuances in the faces of your loved ones and what makes them special and unique to you, such as a certain smile, a freckle, a dimple, a look that speaks volumes, wrinkles, an expresssion, a special eye color or distinct skin tone, a glow, or a certain sparkle in their eyes.

Flowers and portraits of spring also have their own characteristics to showcase their own identity and individuality.

Keep watch on these pages for spring characteristics in flowers and more in tulips, rhododendrons, daffodils, irises, pansies, magnolias, hyacinths, lilacs, columbines, dandelions, many other flowers, tree blossoms, pine trees, rain, new leaves, seed pods, and grass.

By celebrating each individual portrait of spring, we honor and acknowledge the new beginnings in nature as well as the new beginnings in our life. Open your eyes to see the beauty and life around you.

Thank you for picking up this book and experiencing these portraits together.

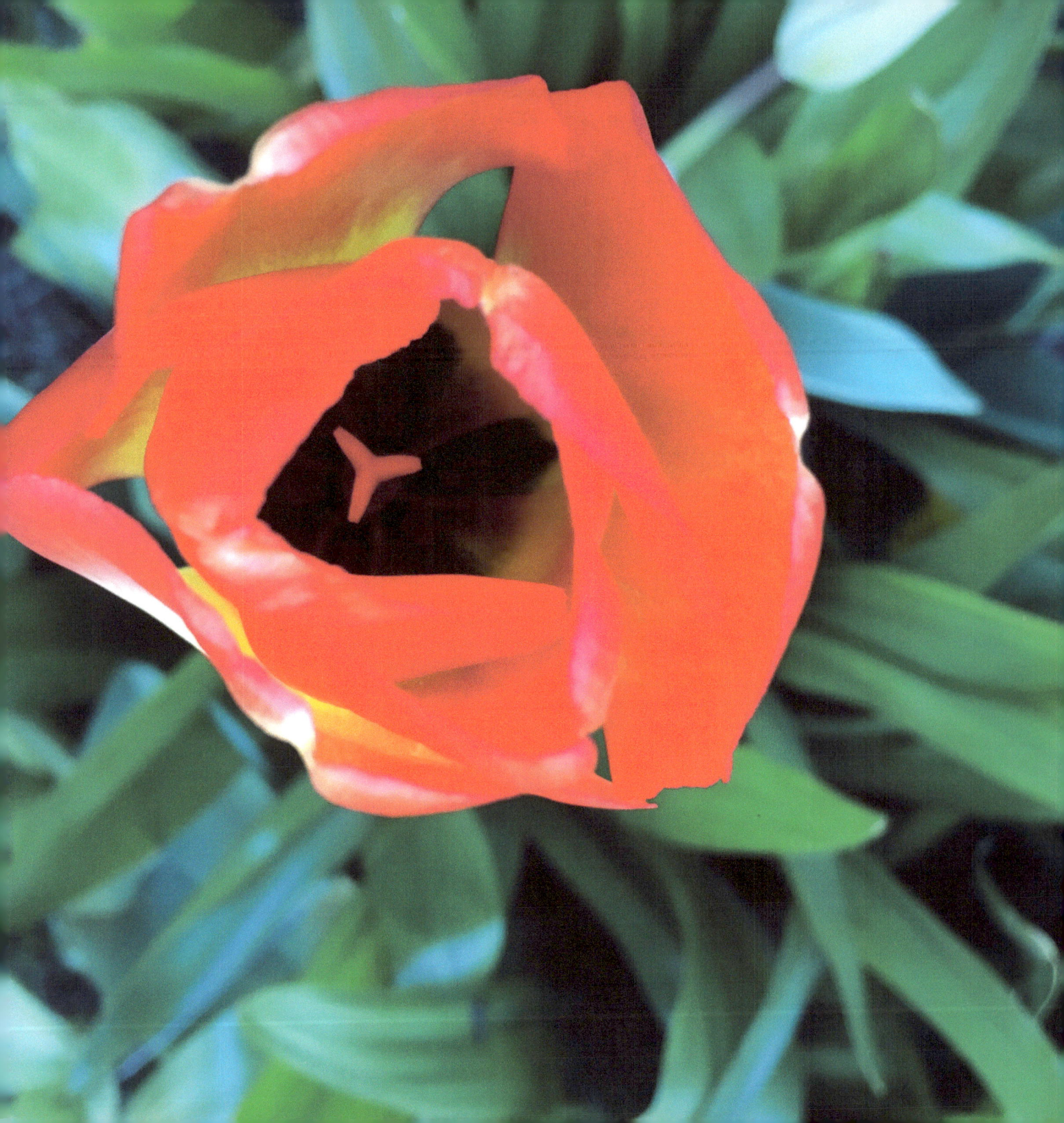

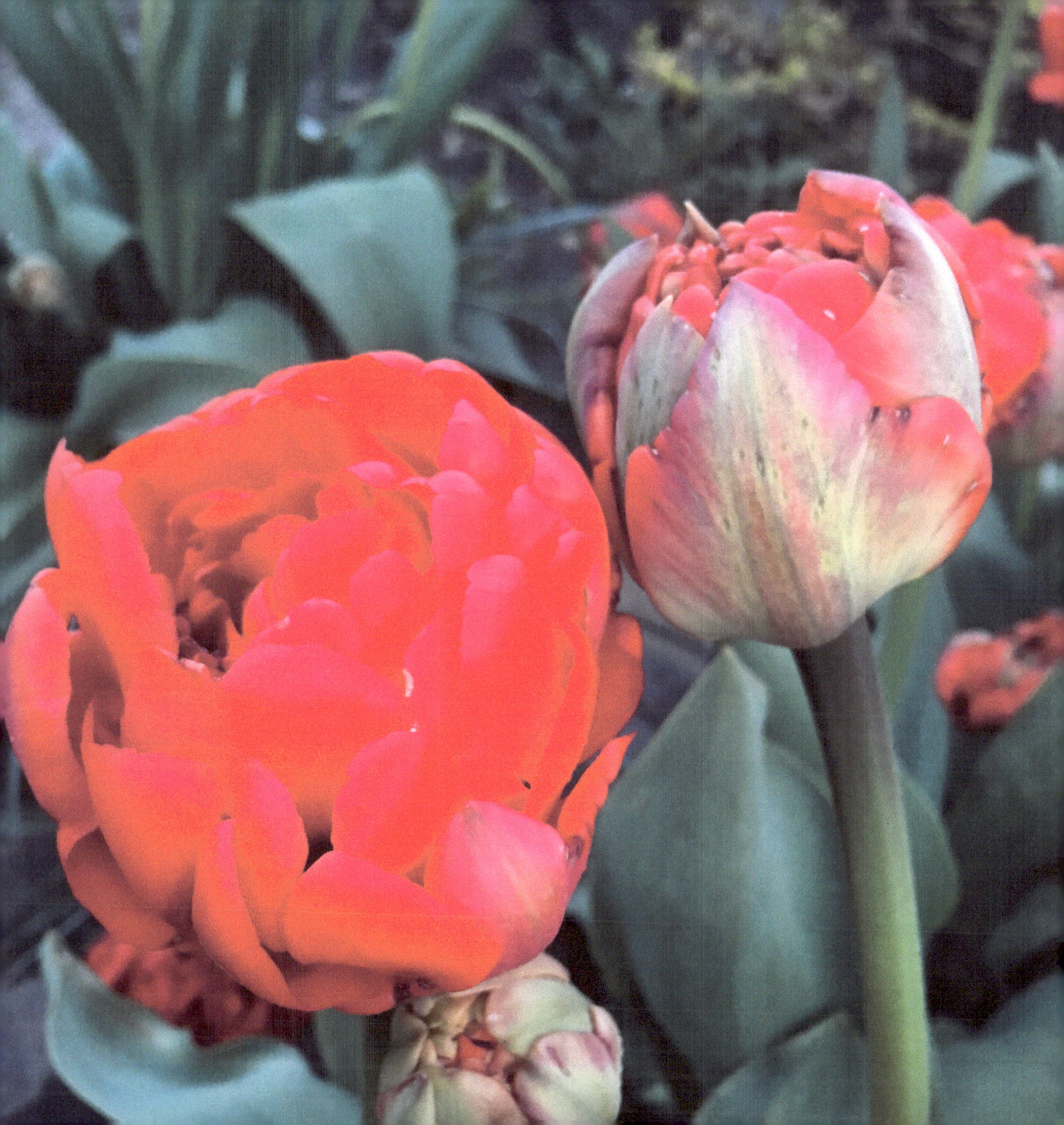

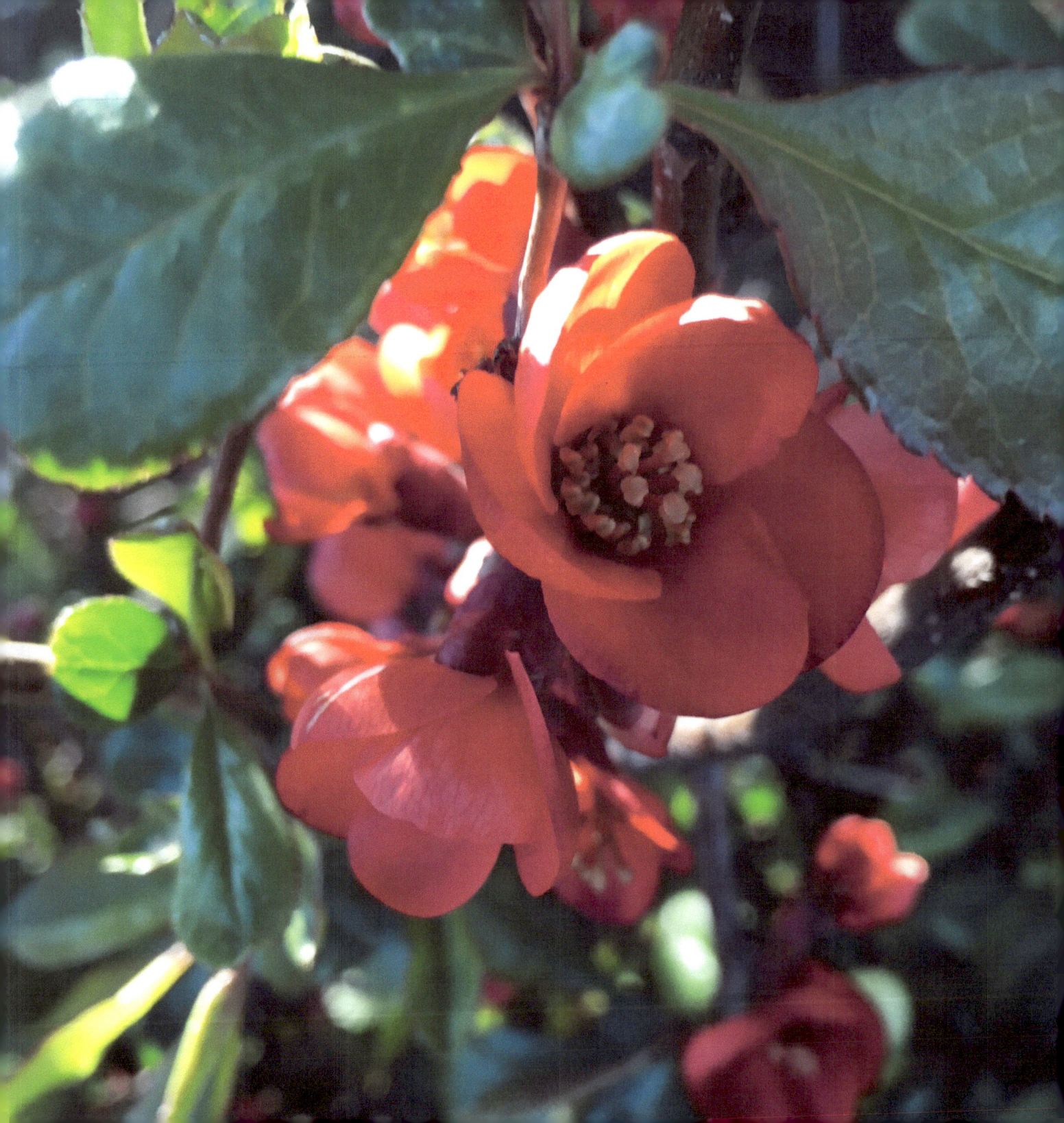

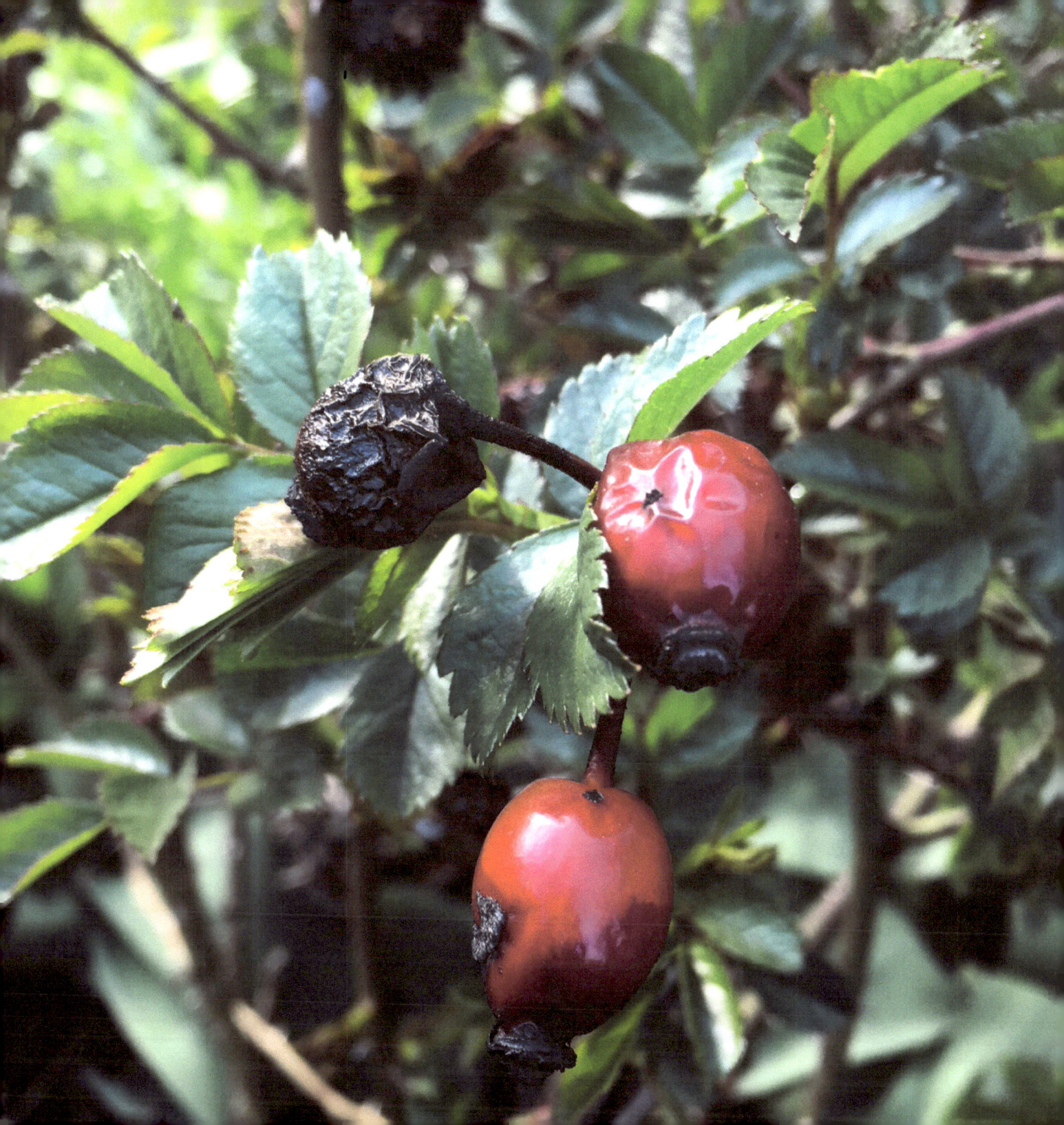

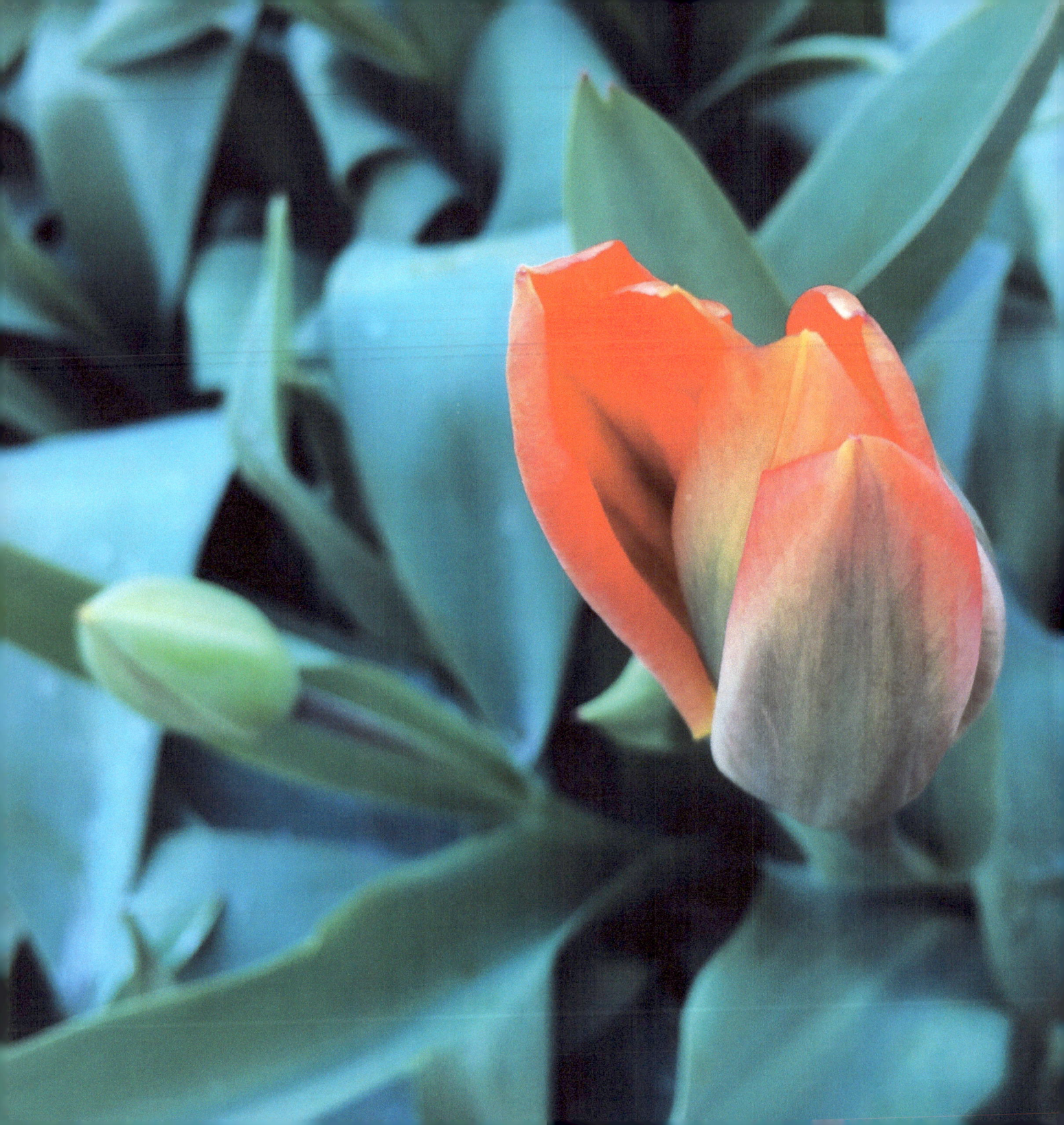

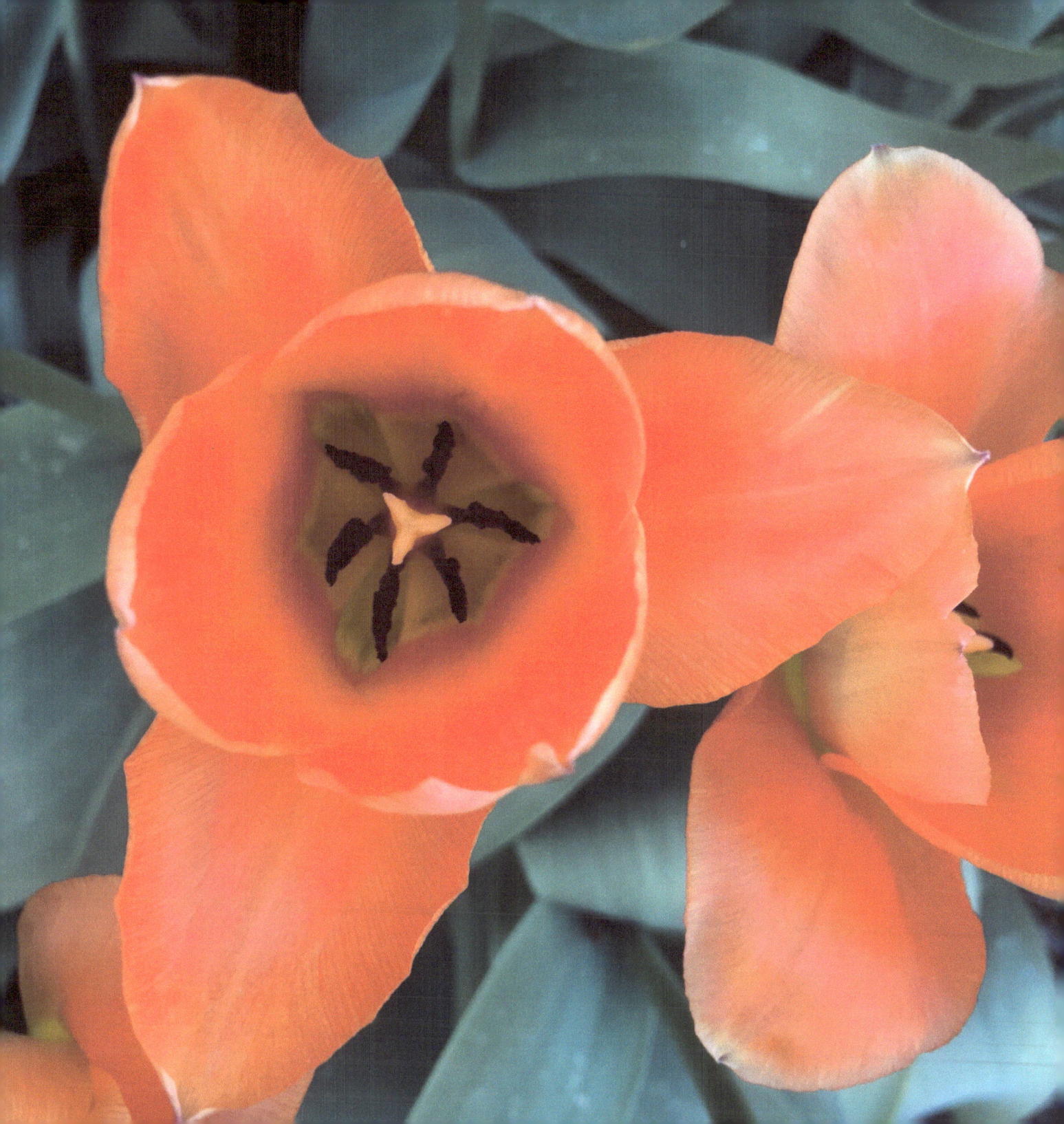

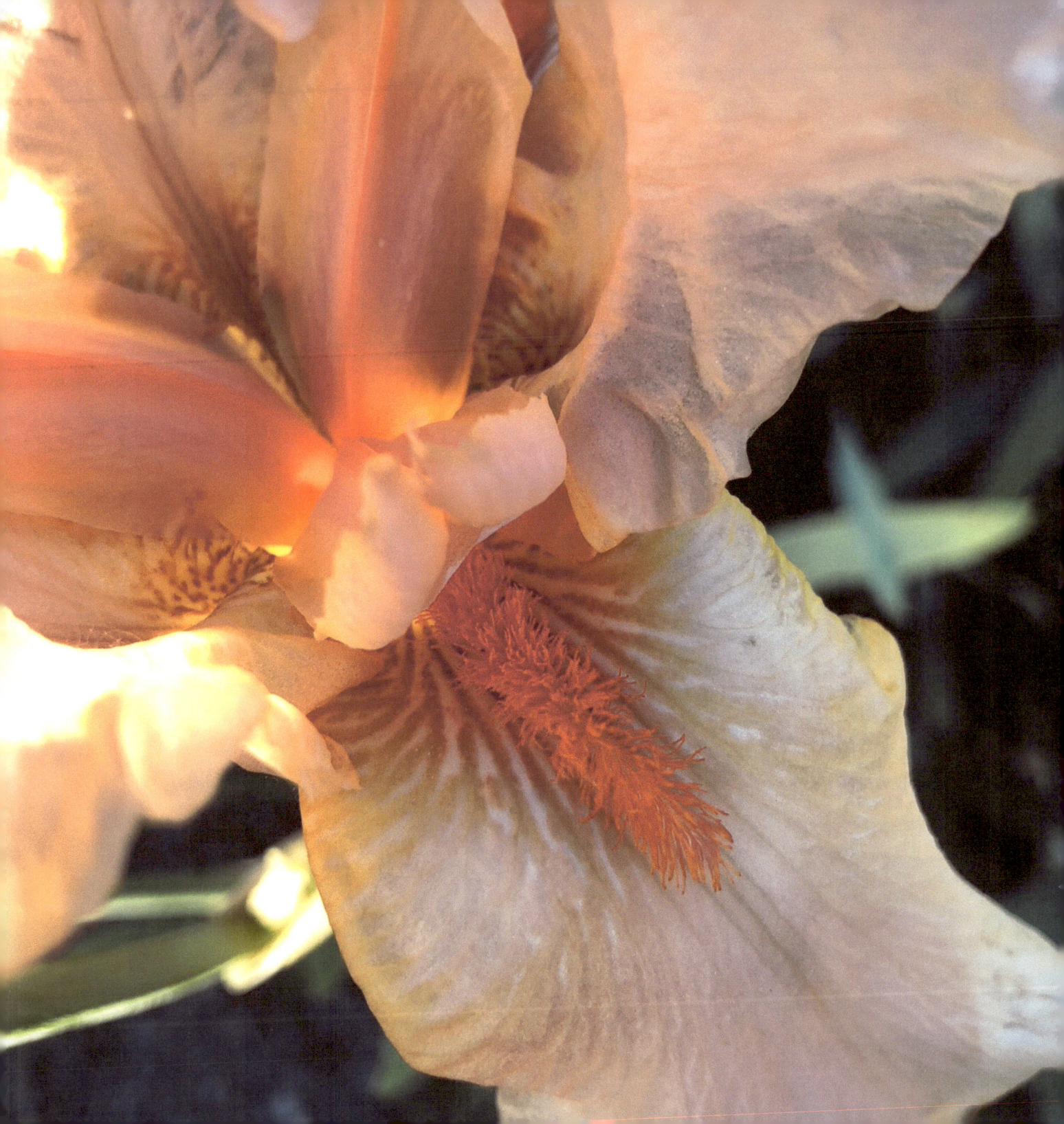

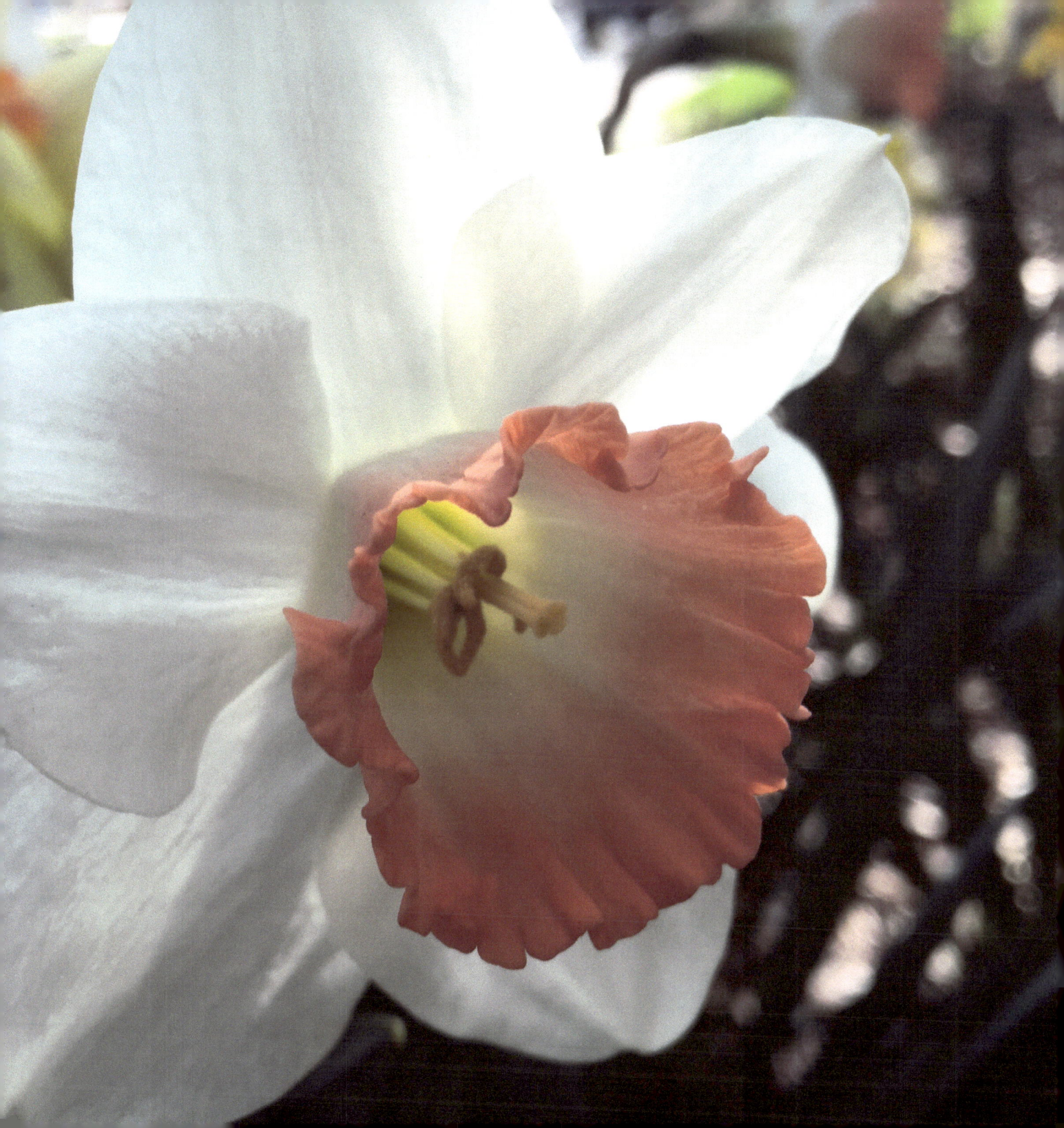

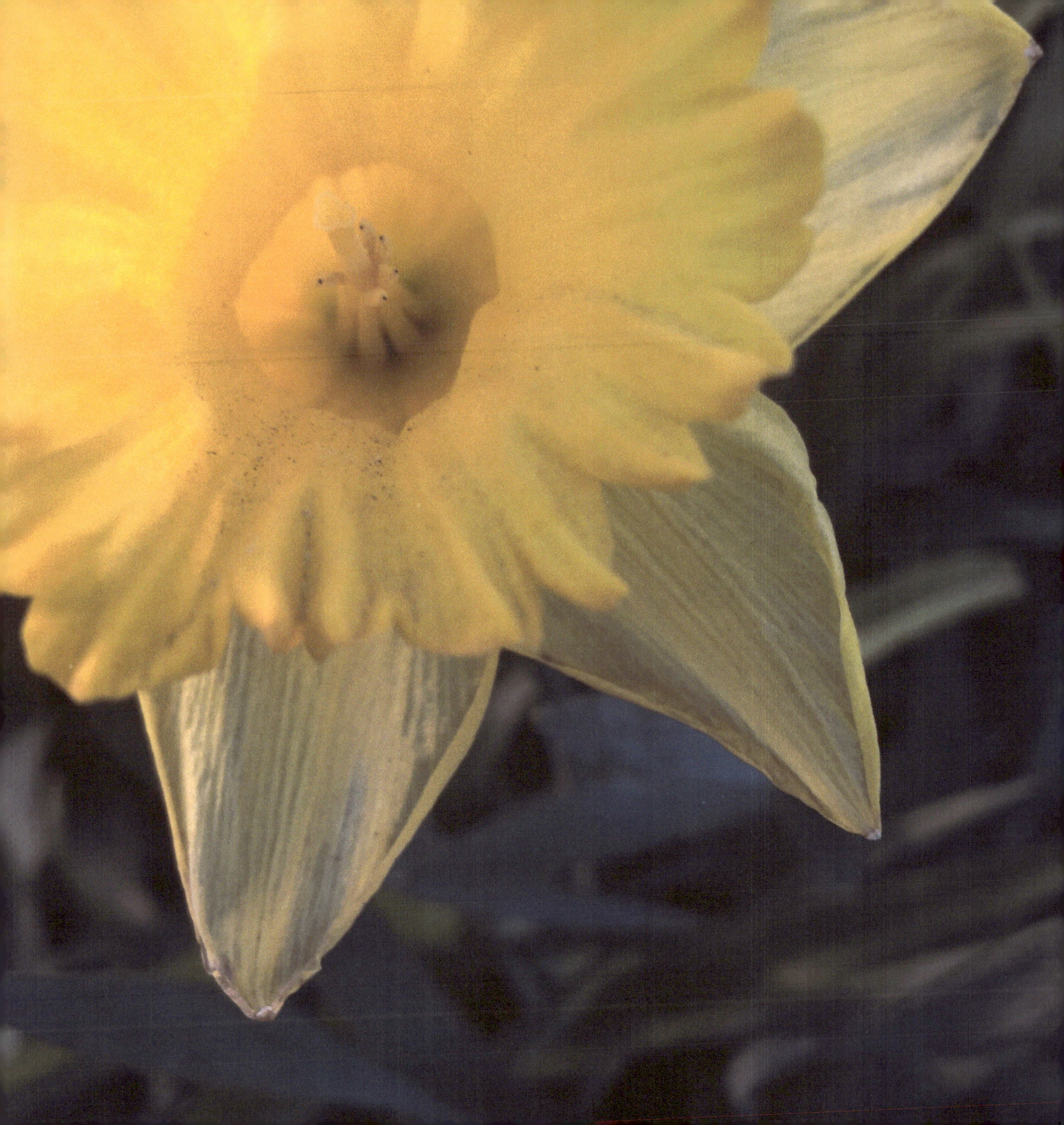

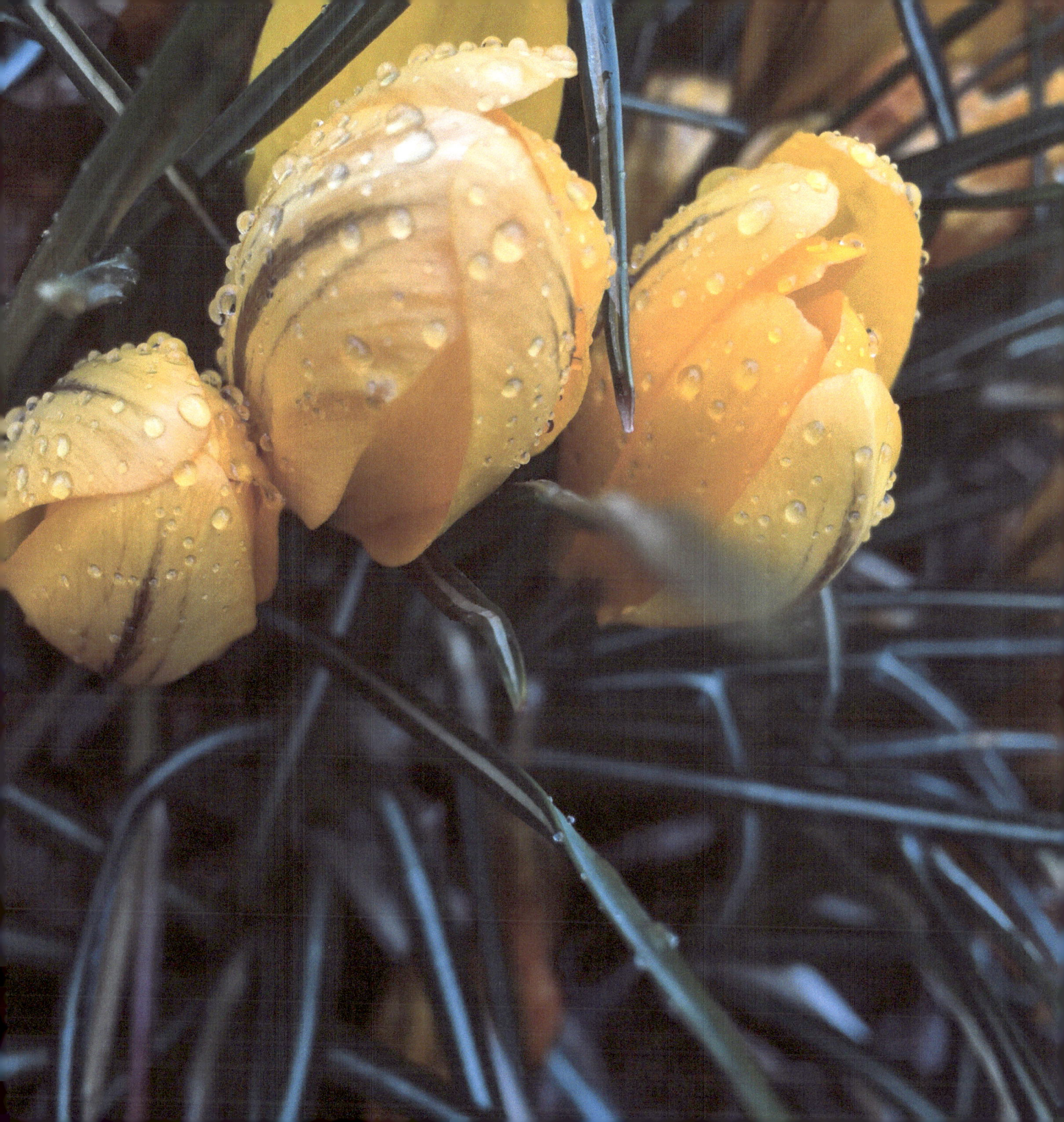

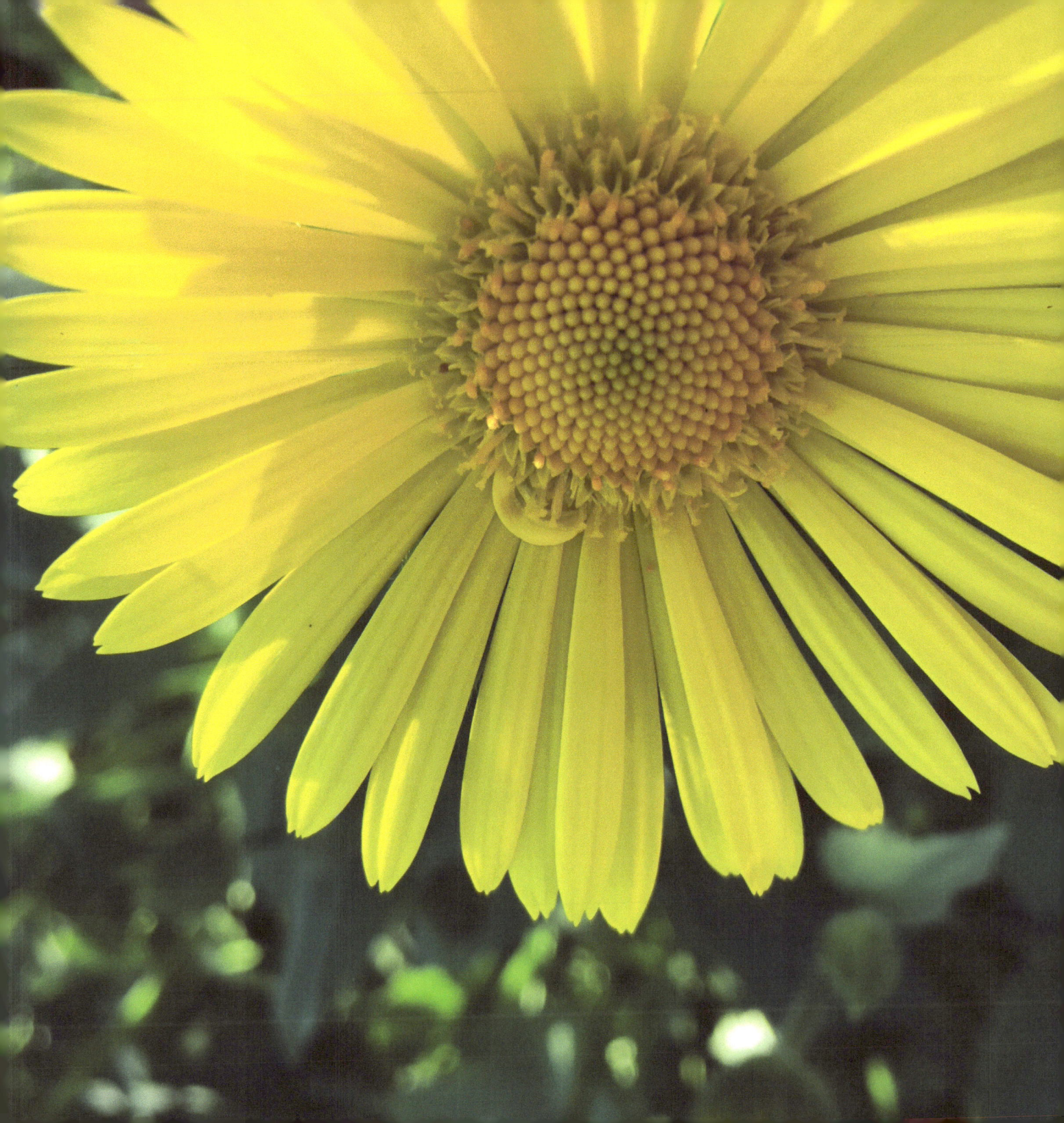

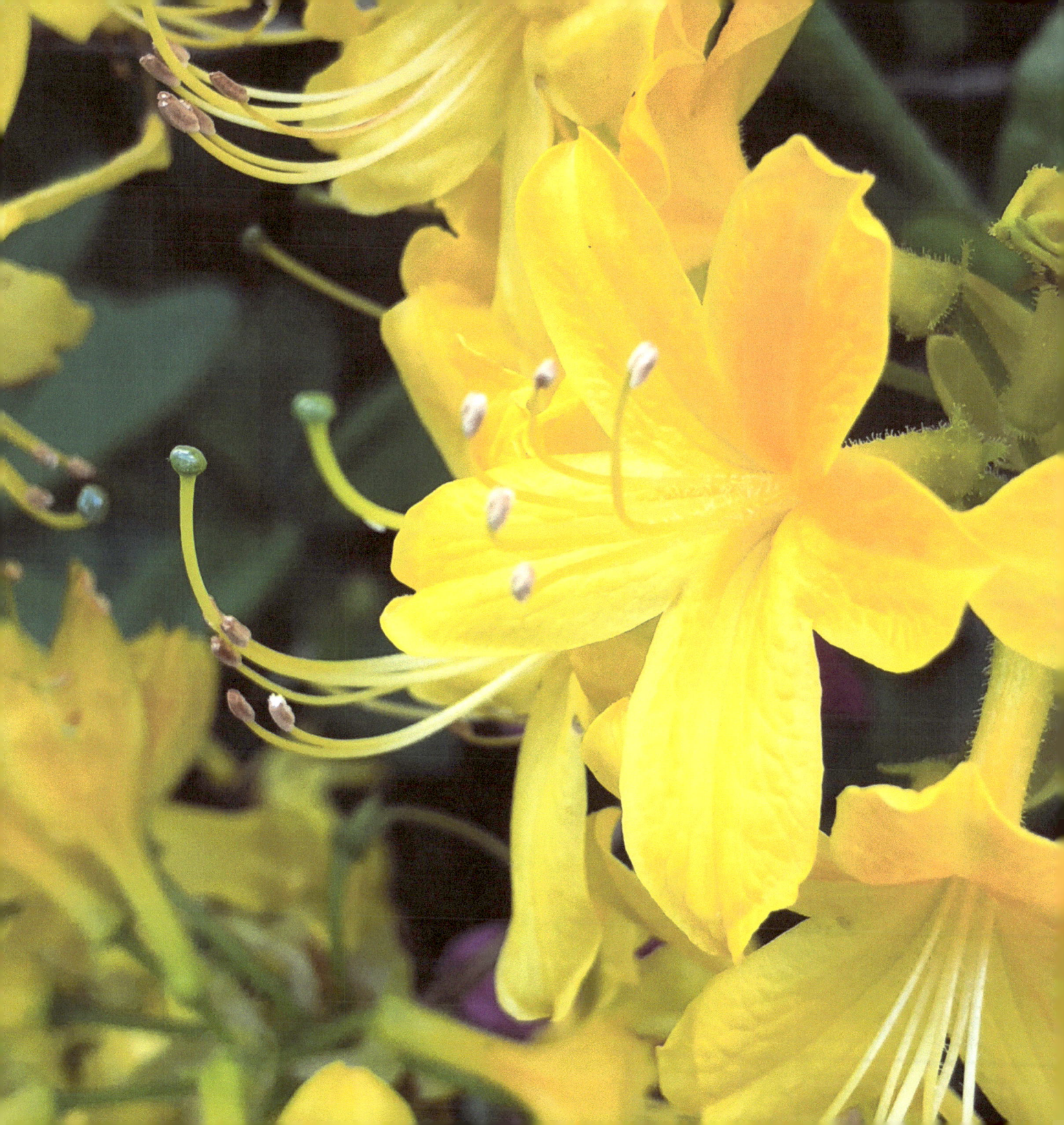

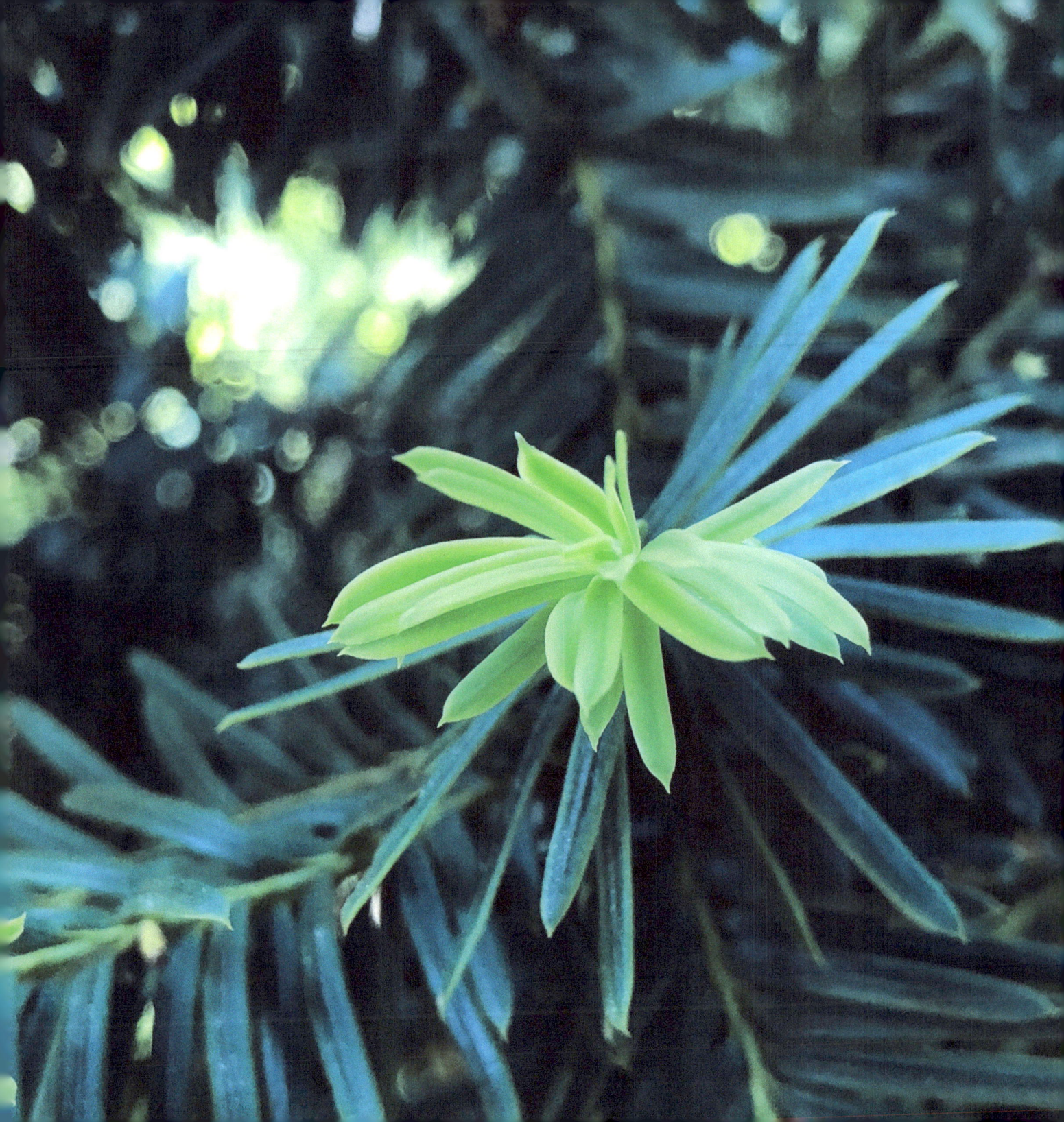

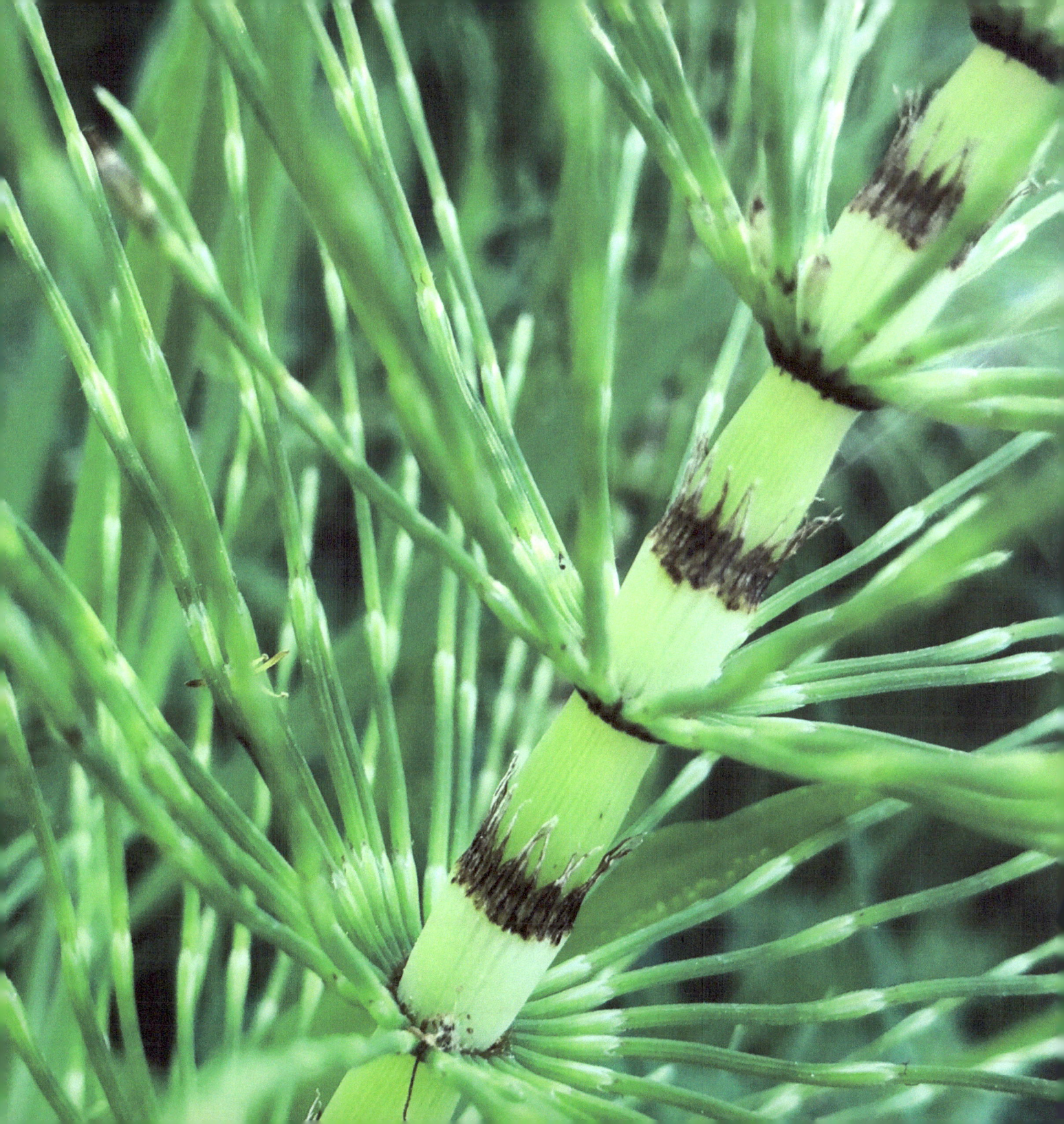

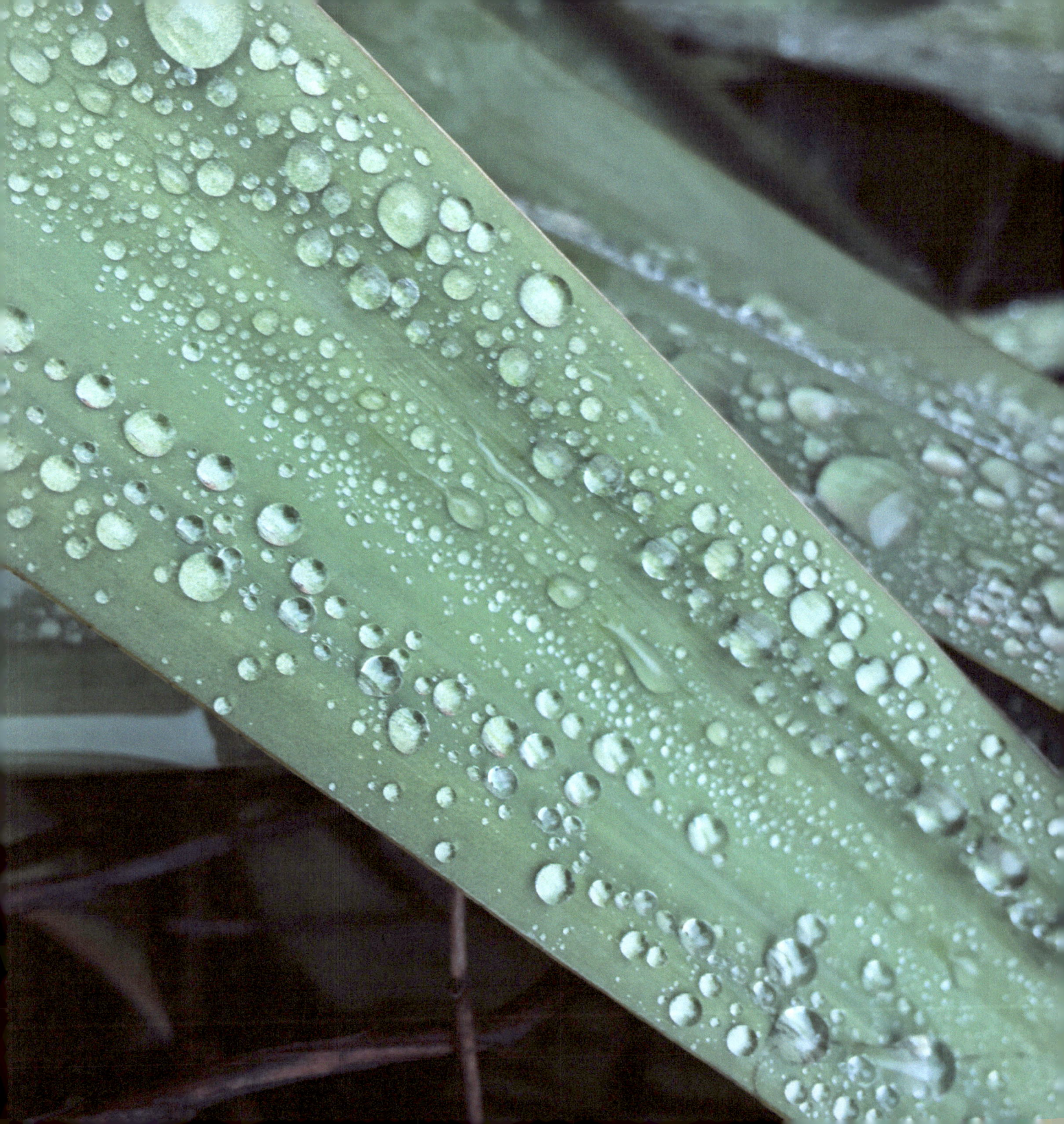

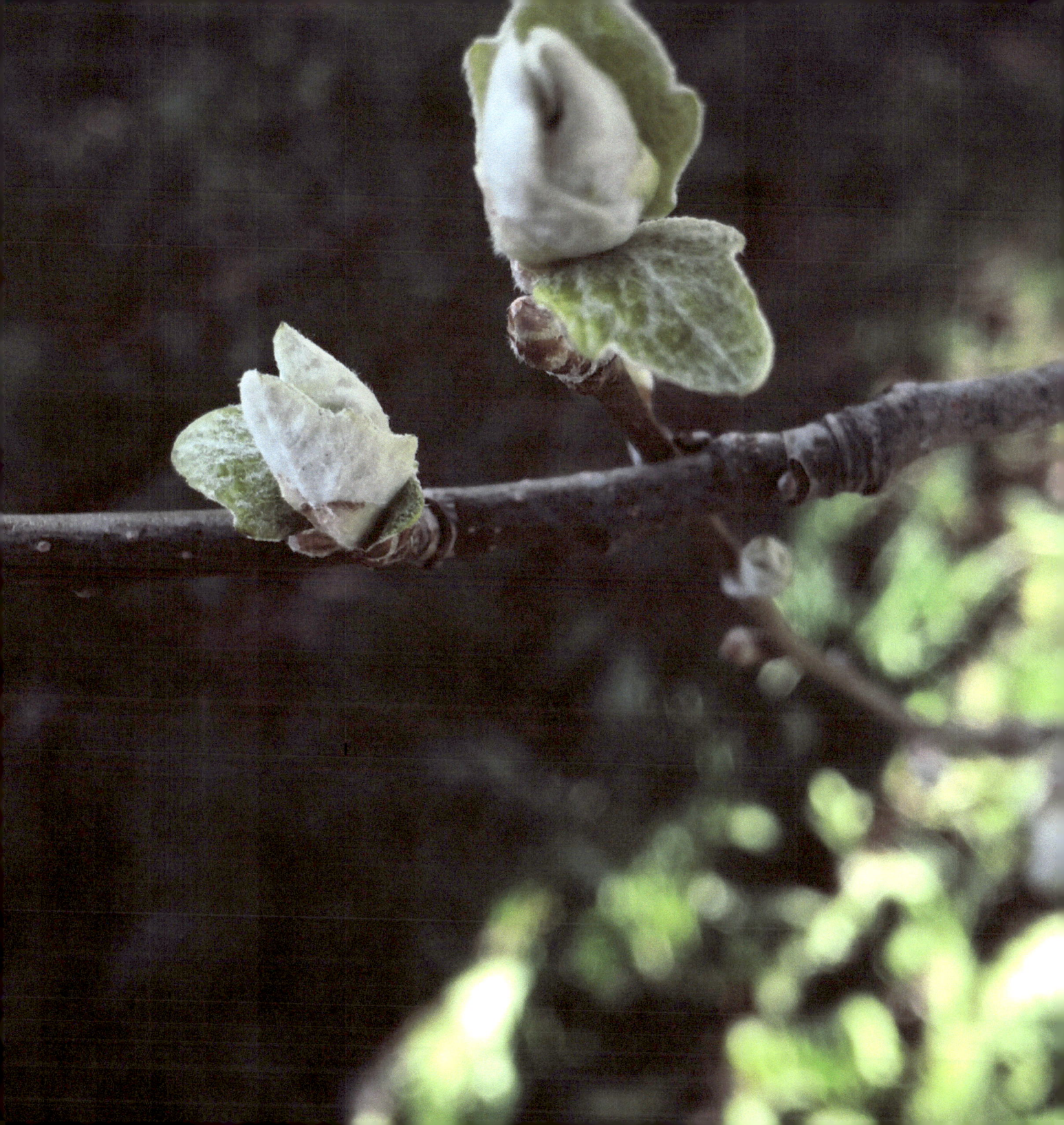

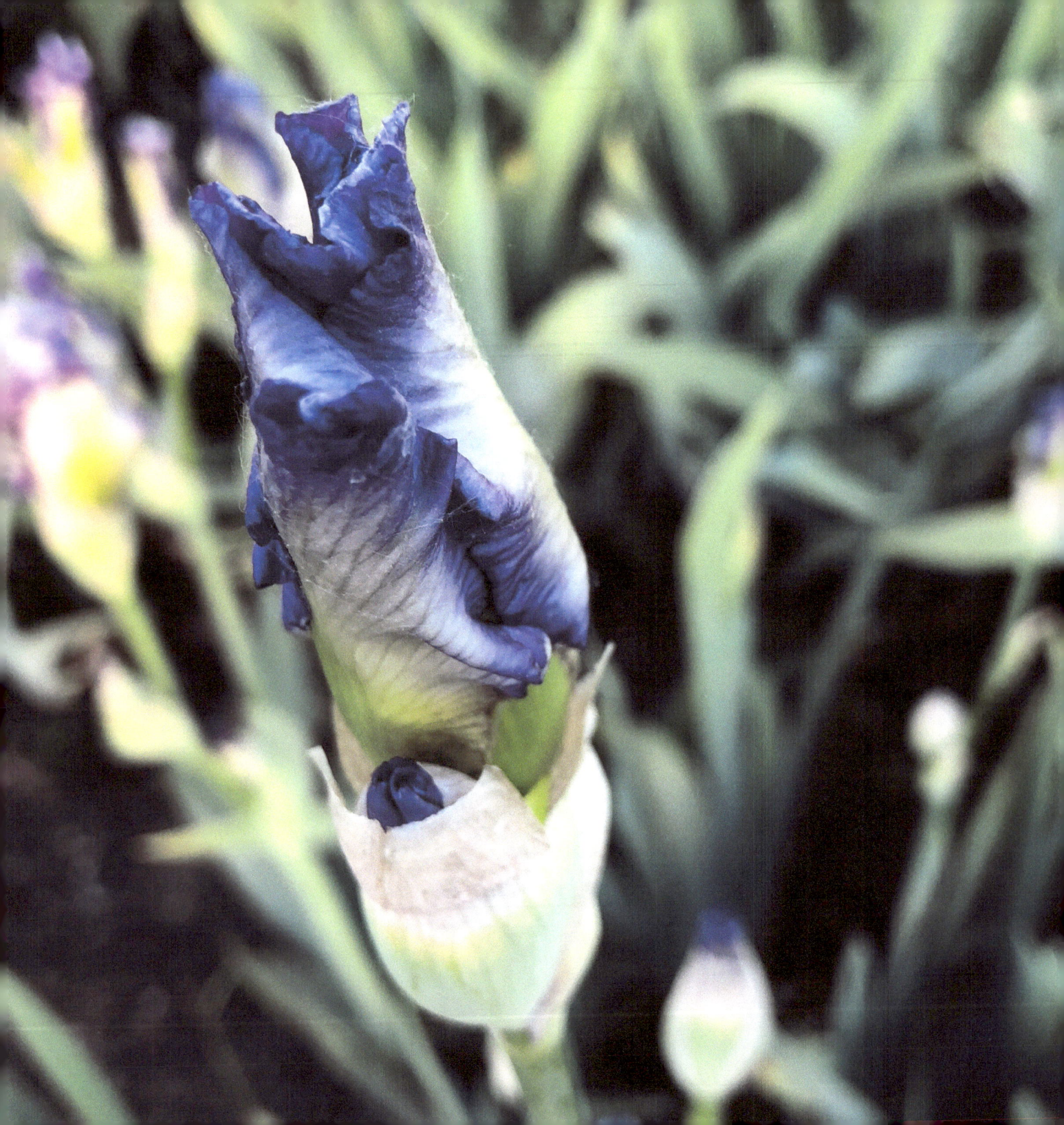

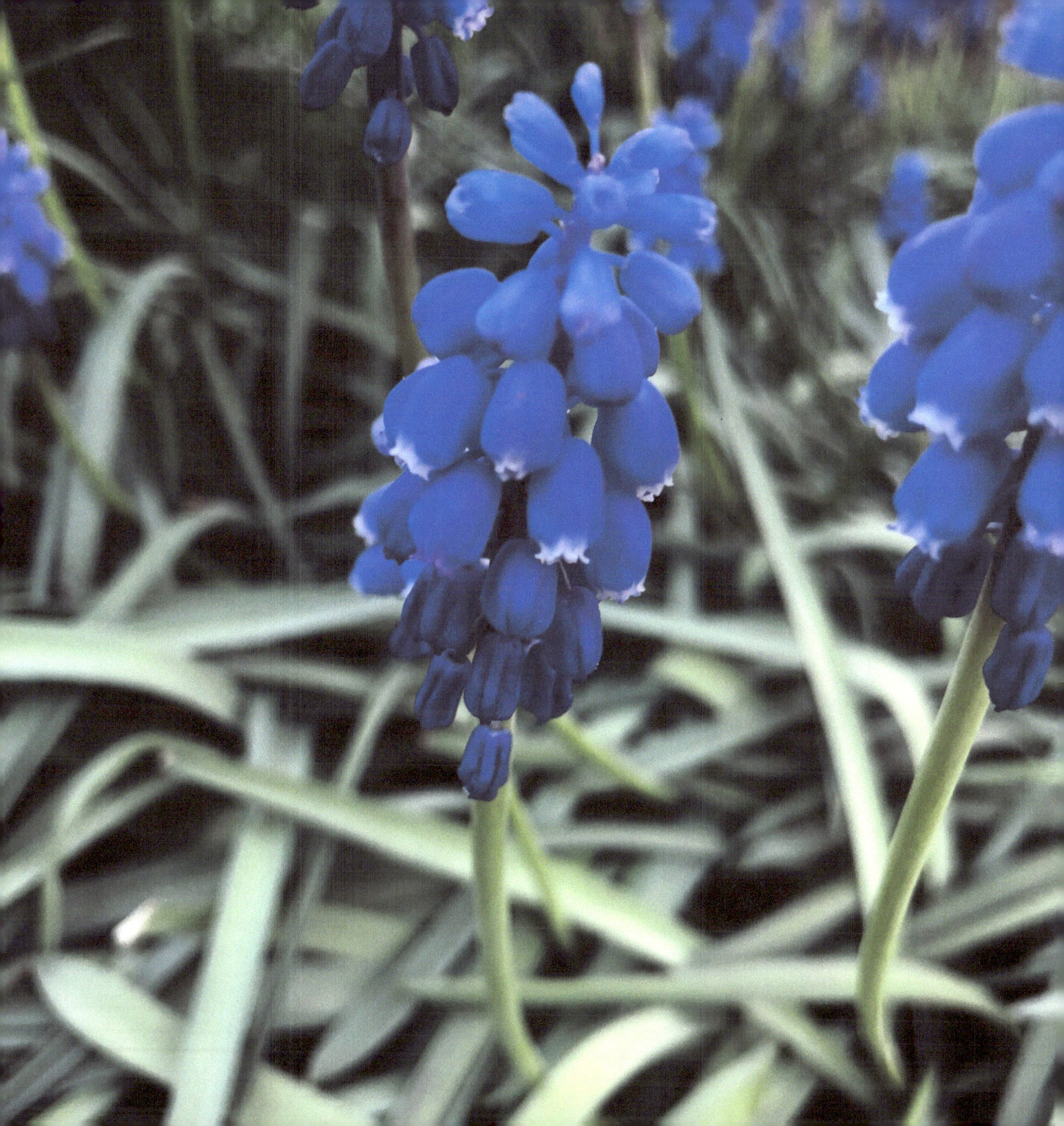

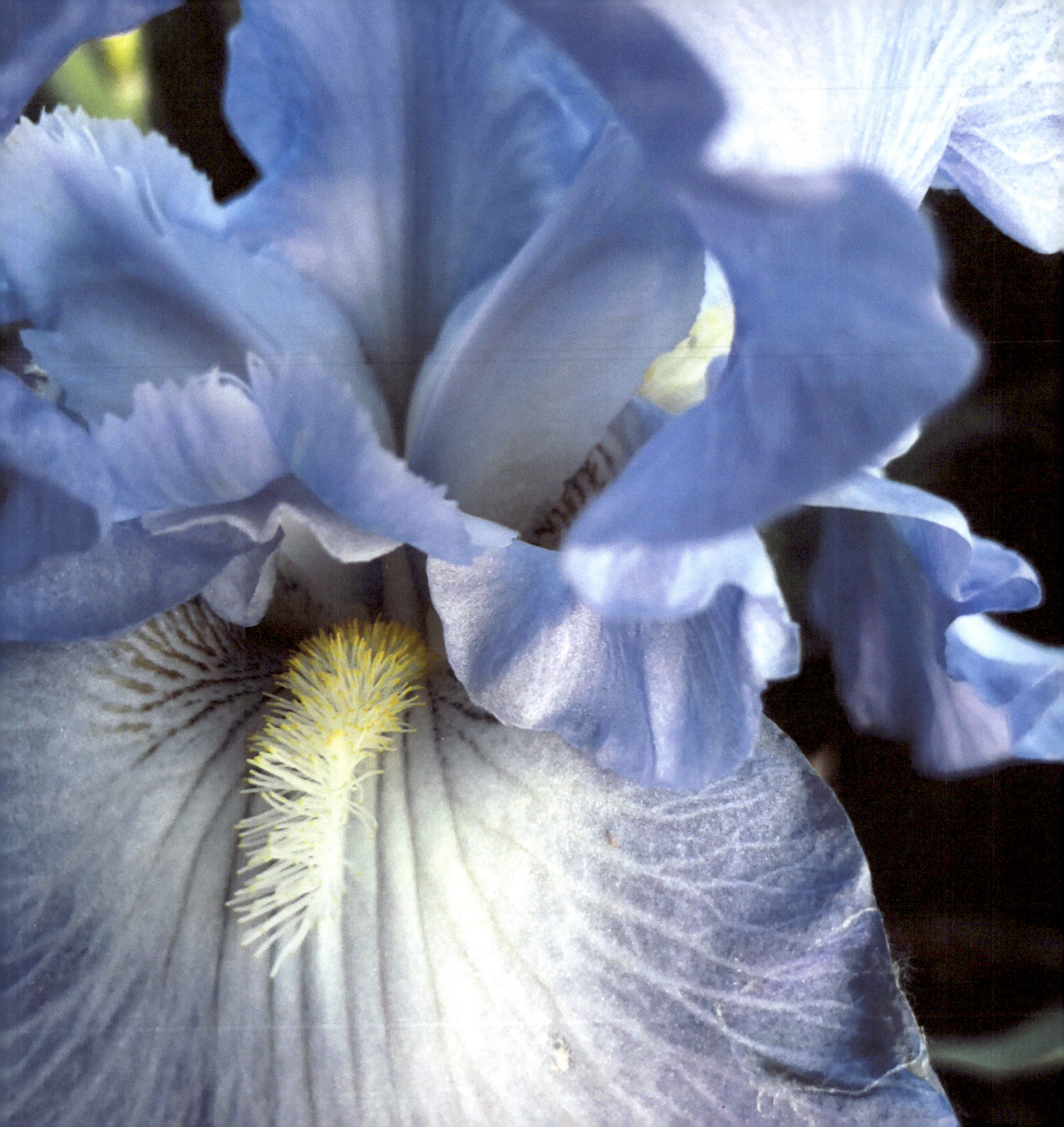

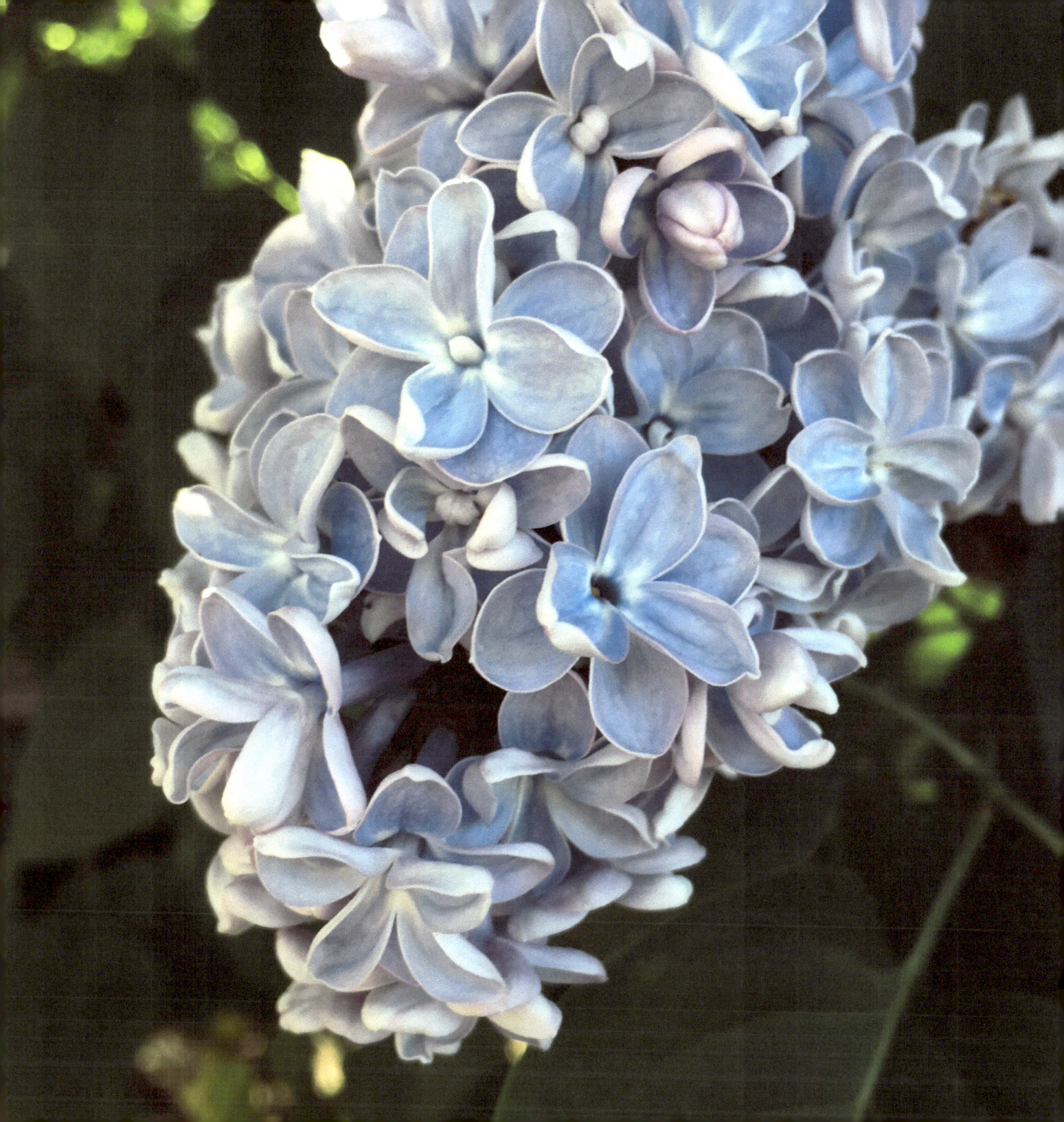

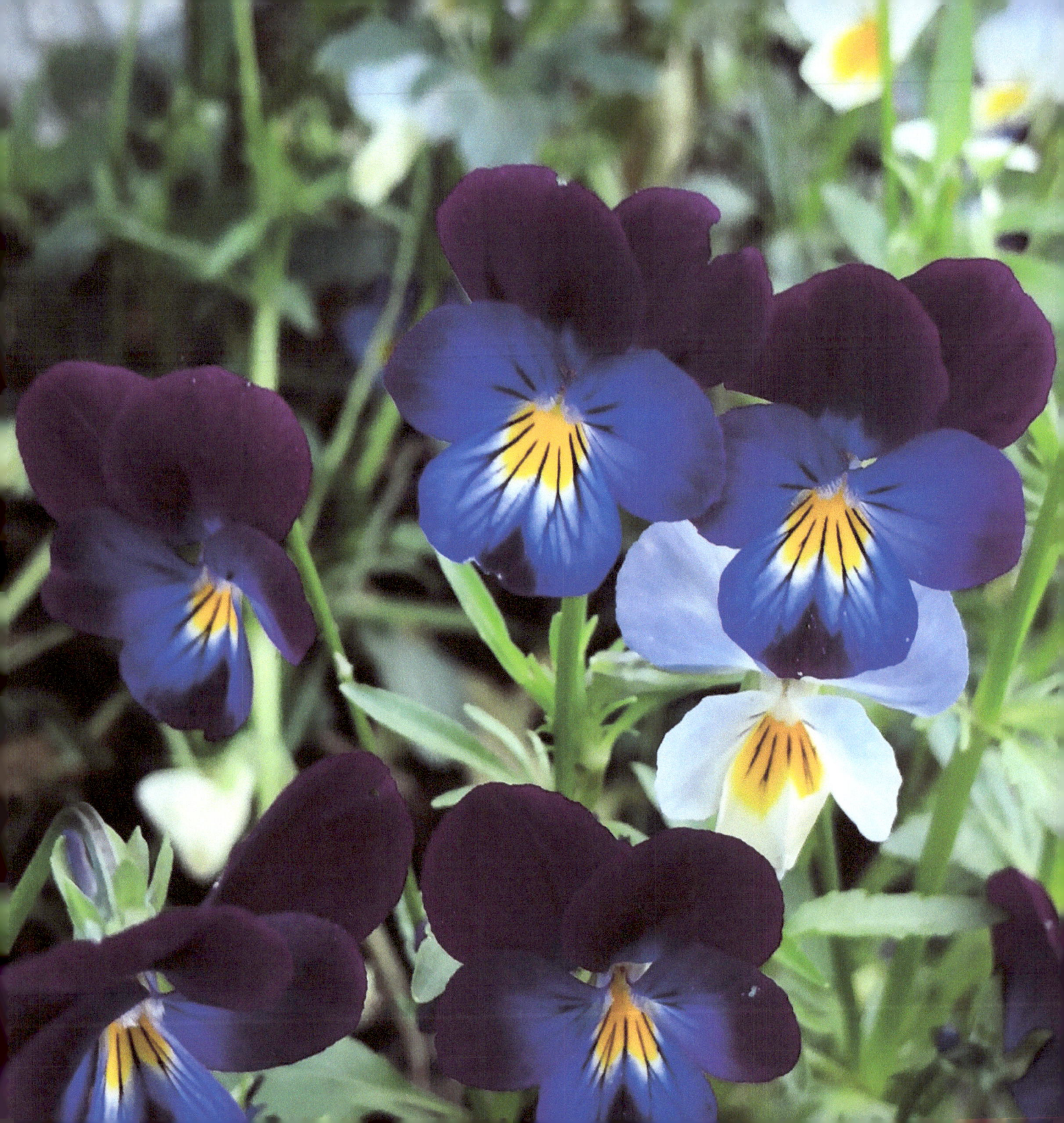

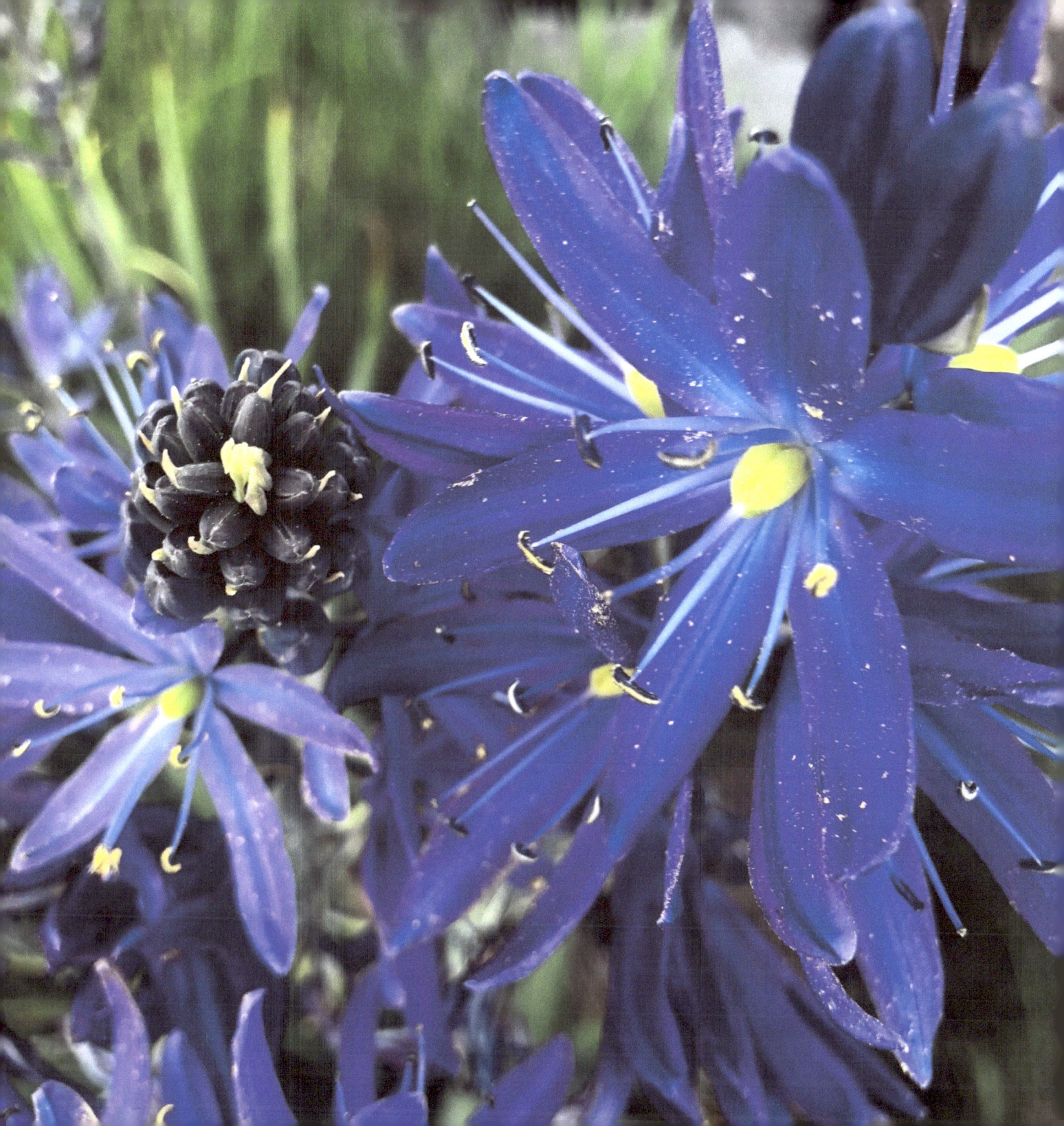

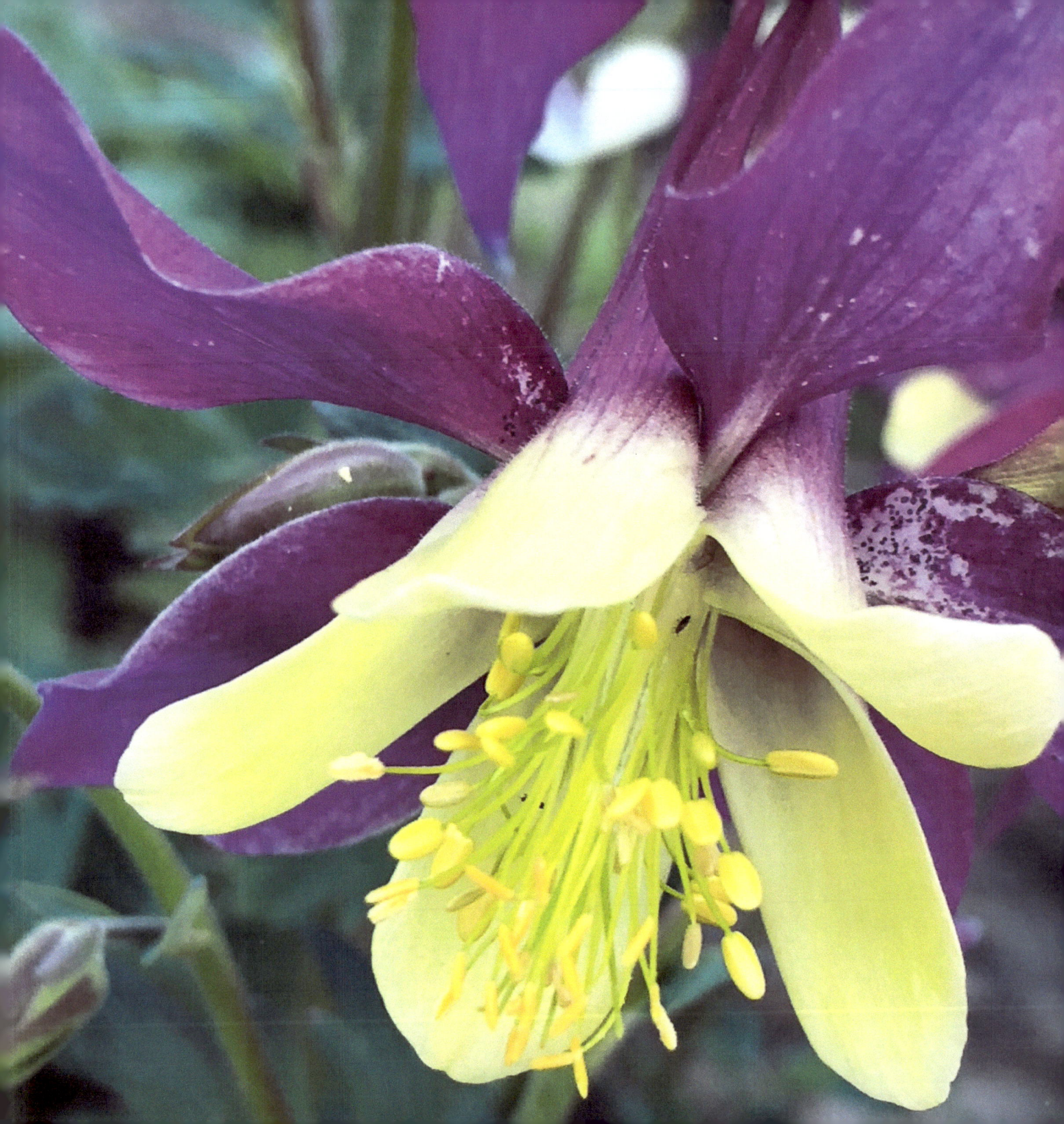

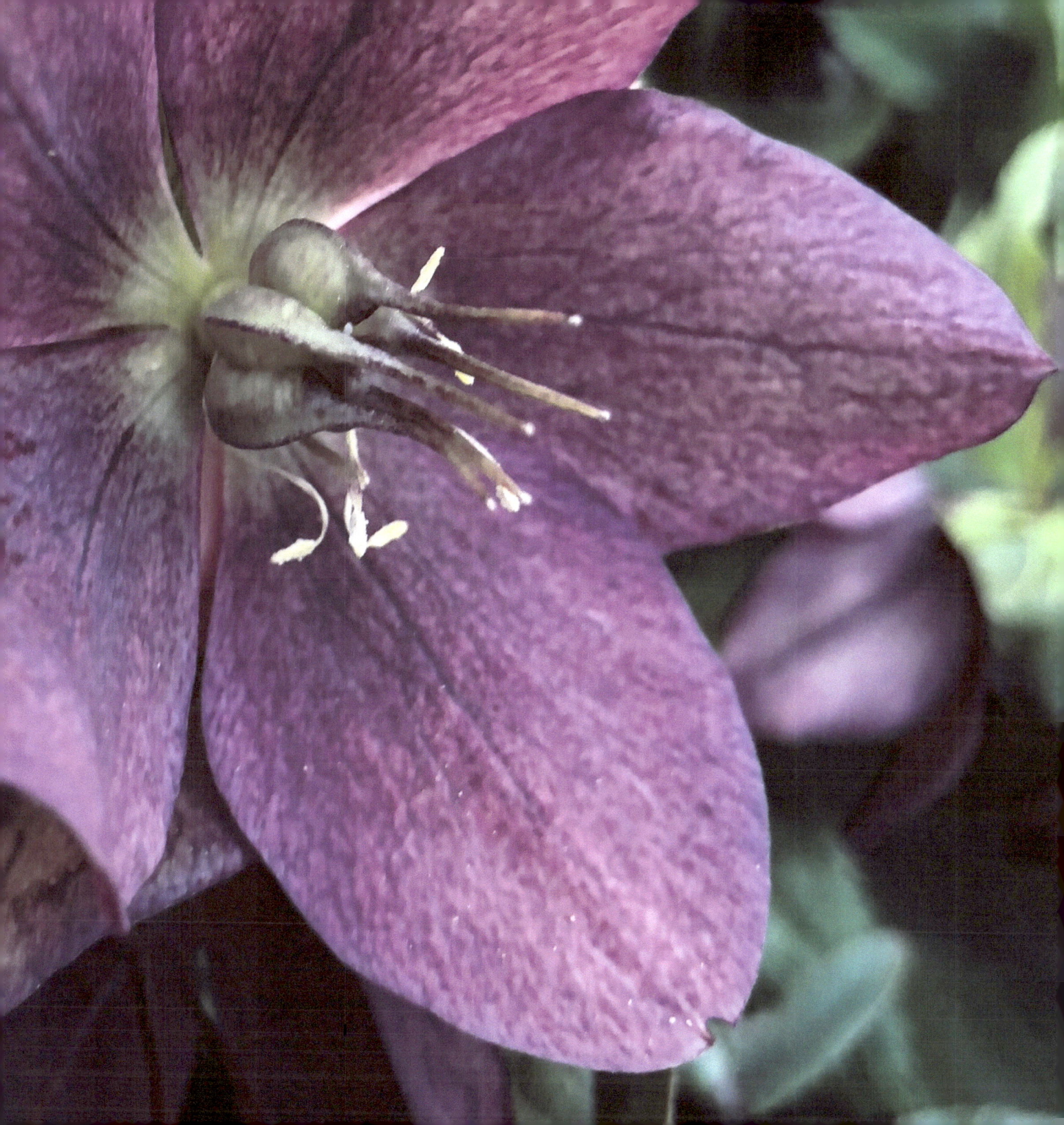

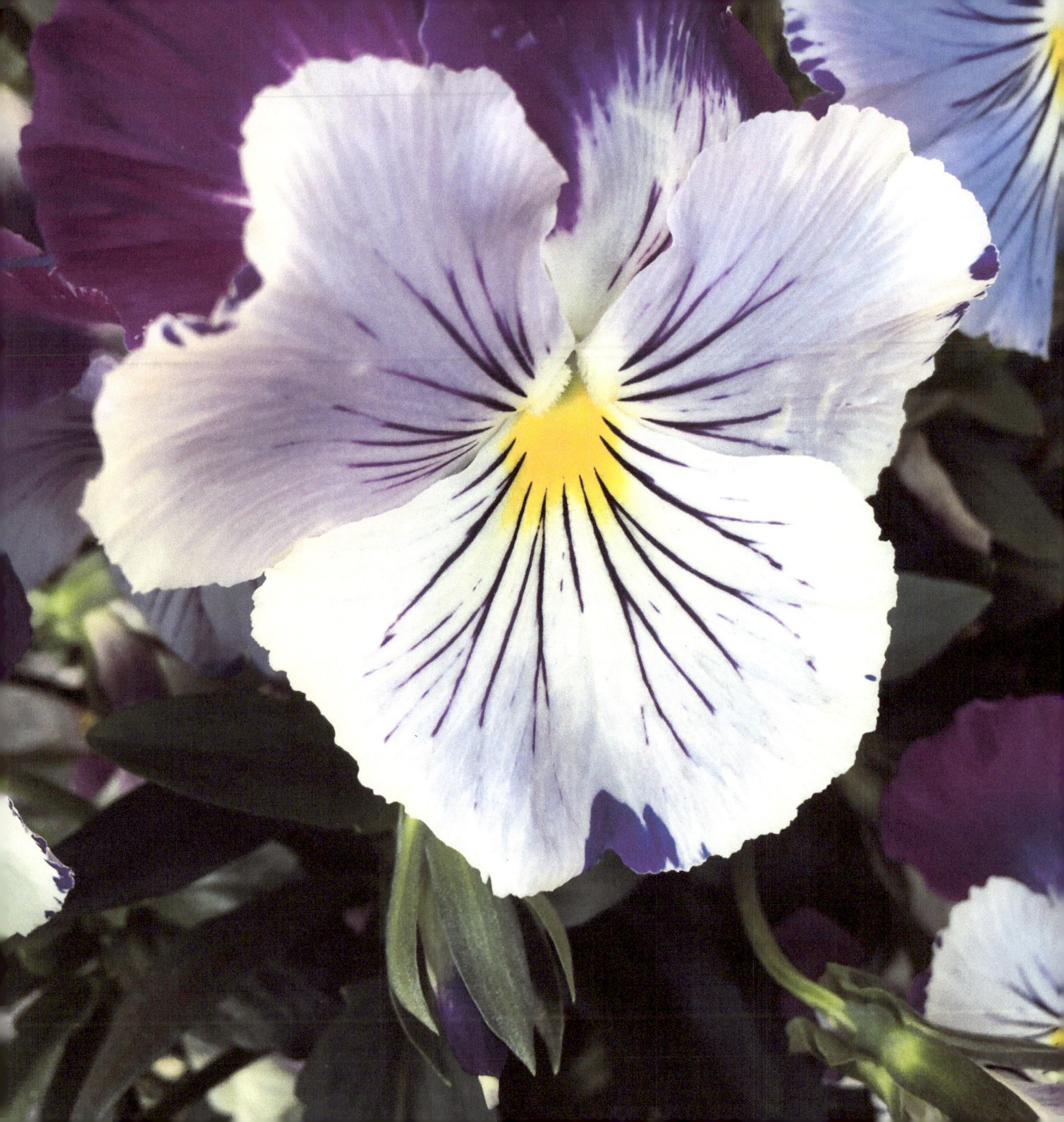

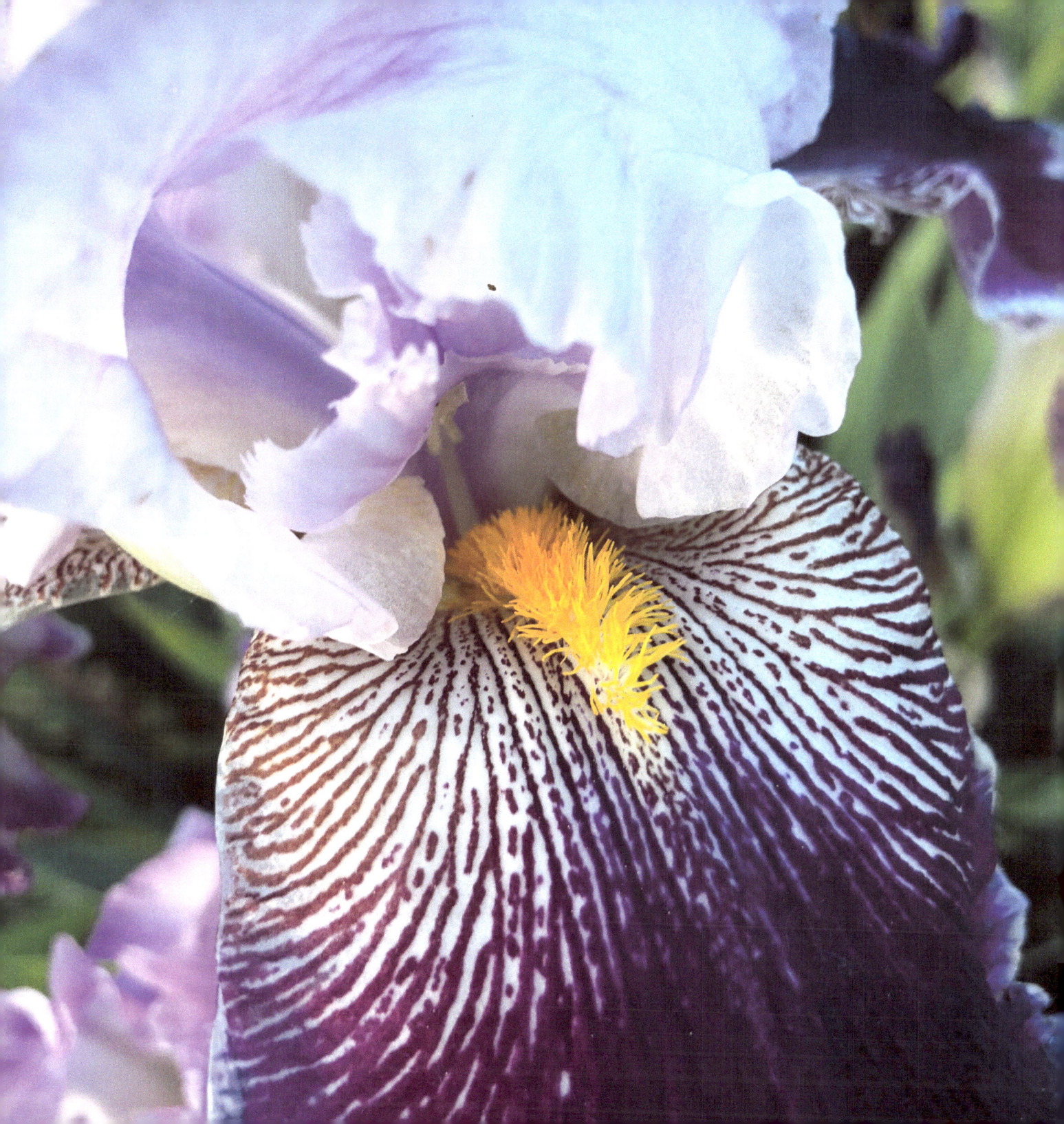

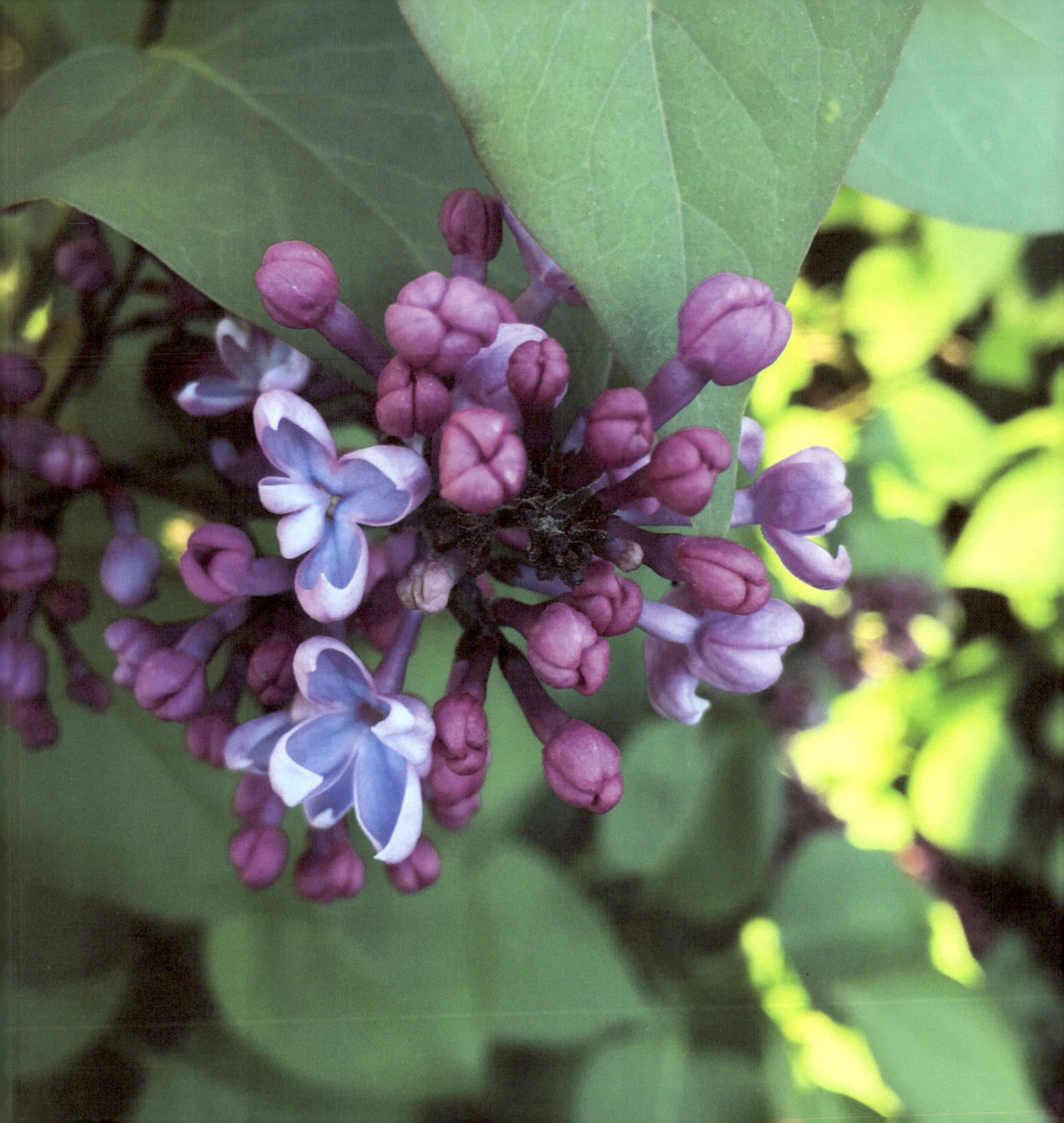

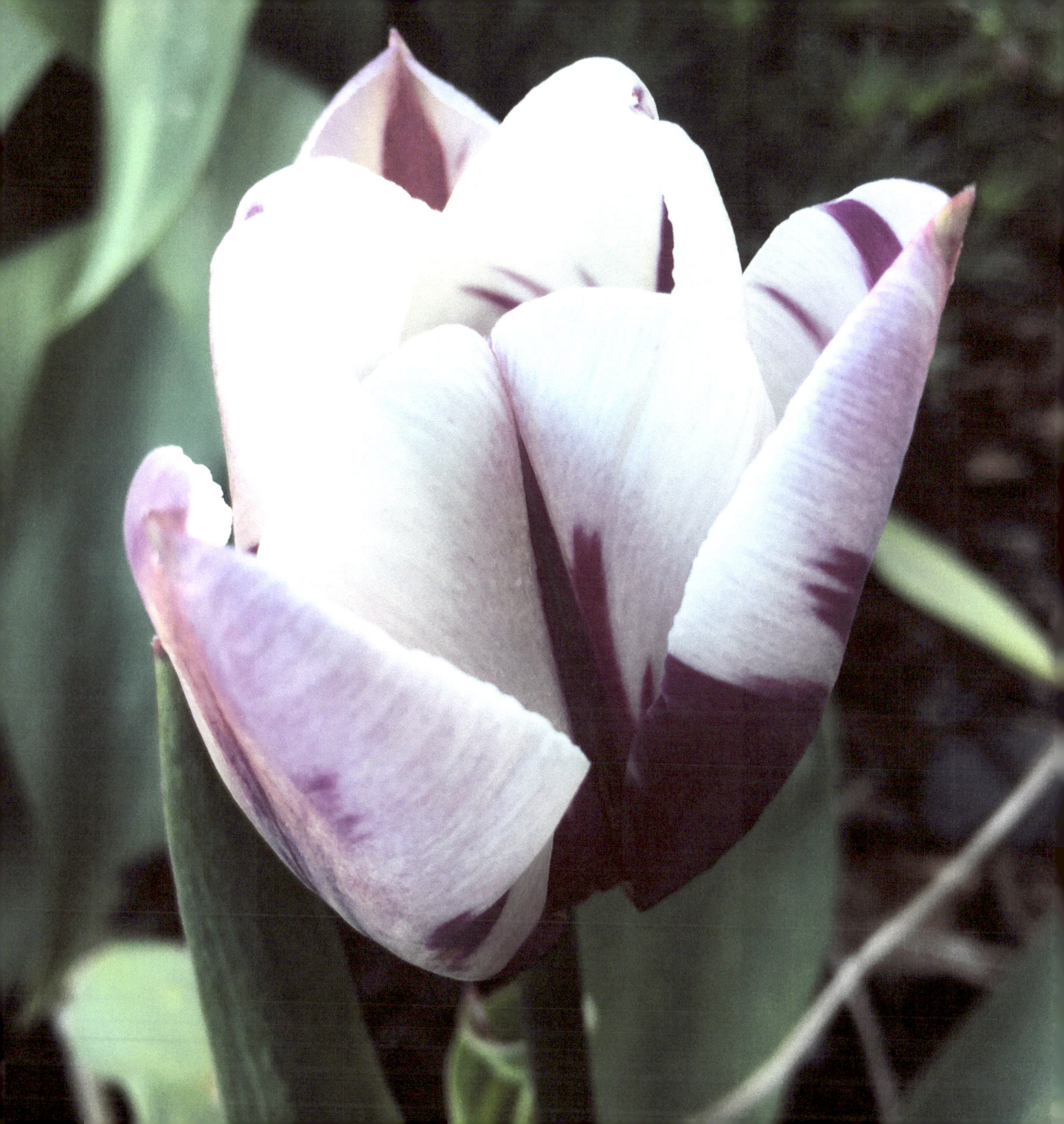

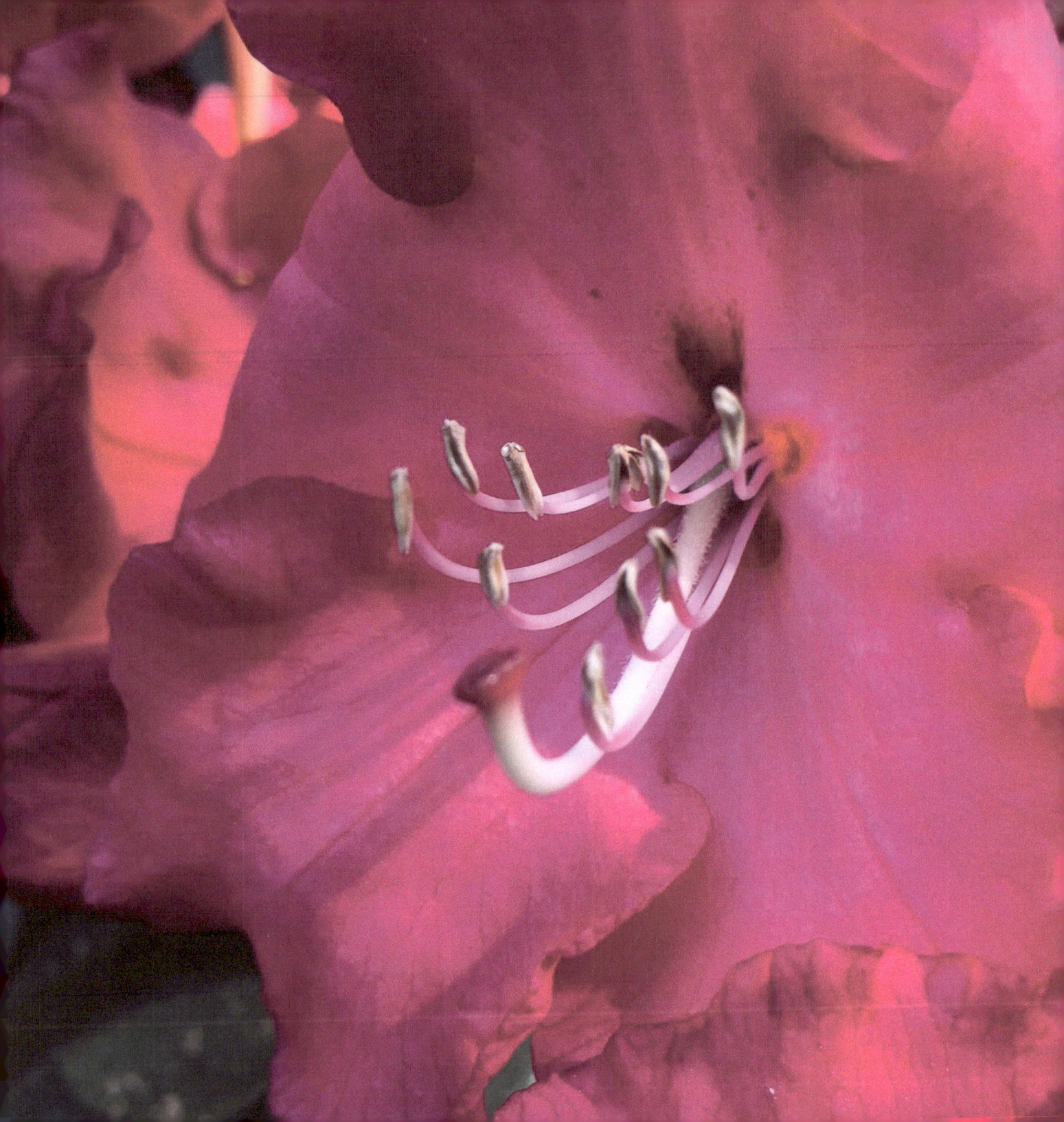

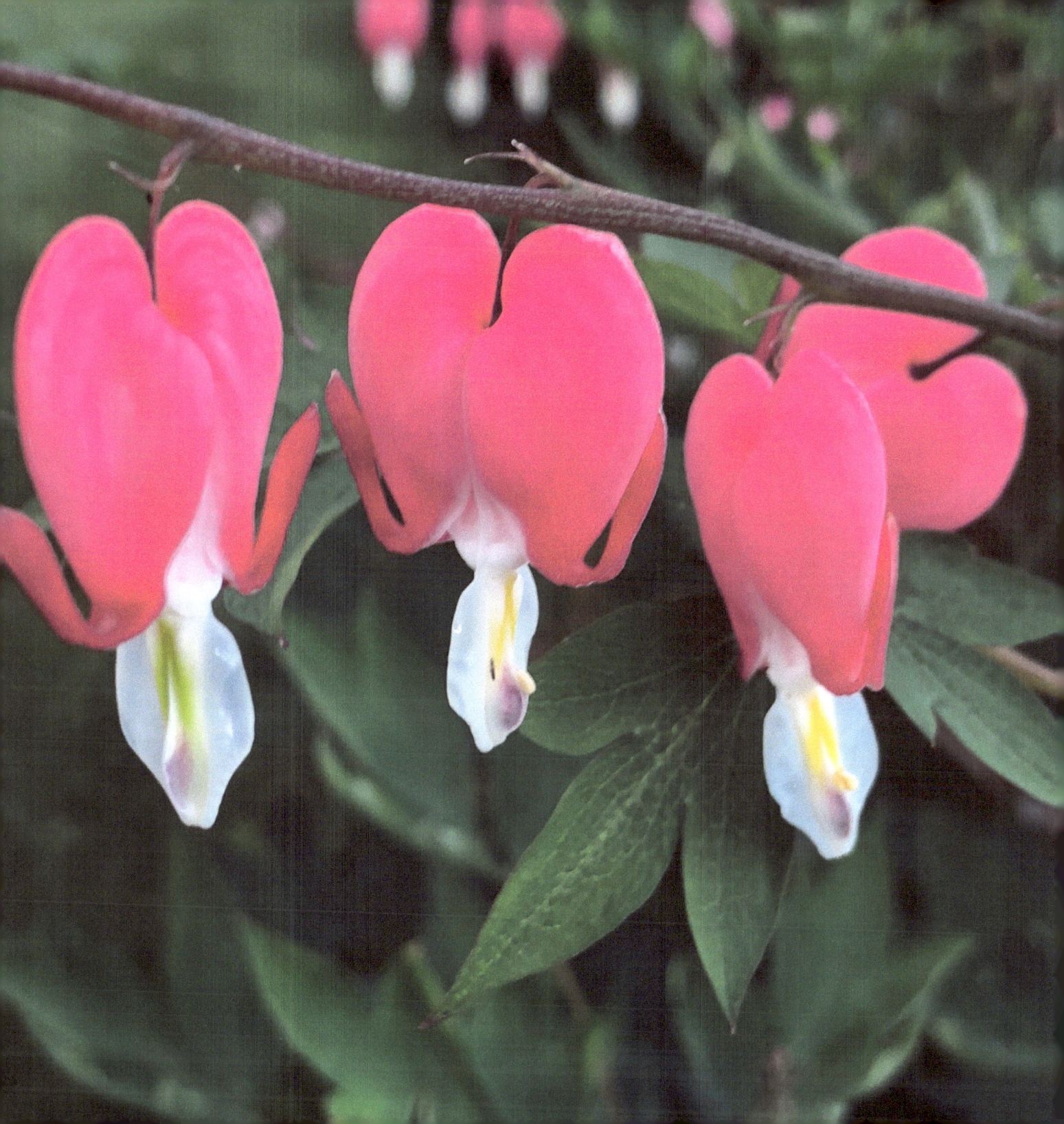

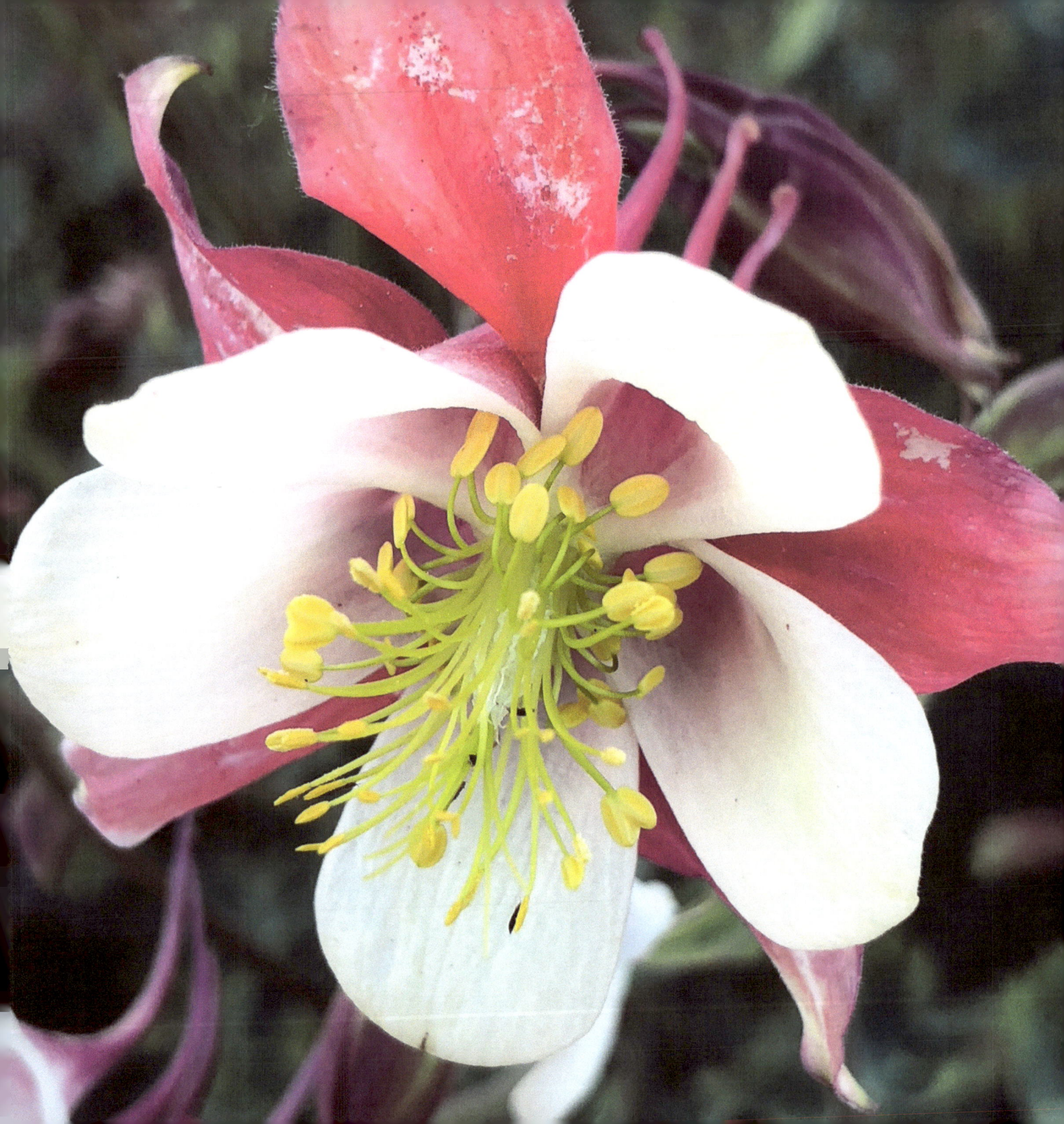

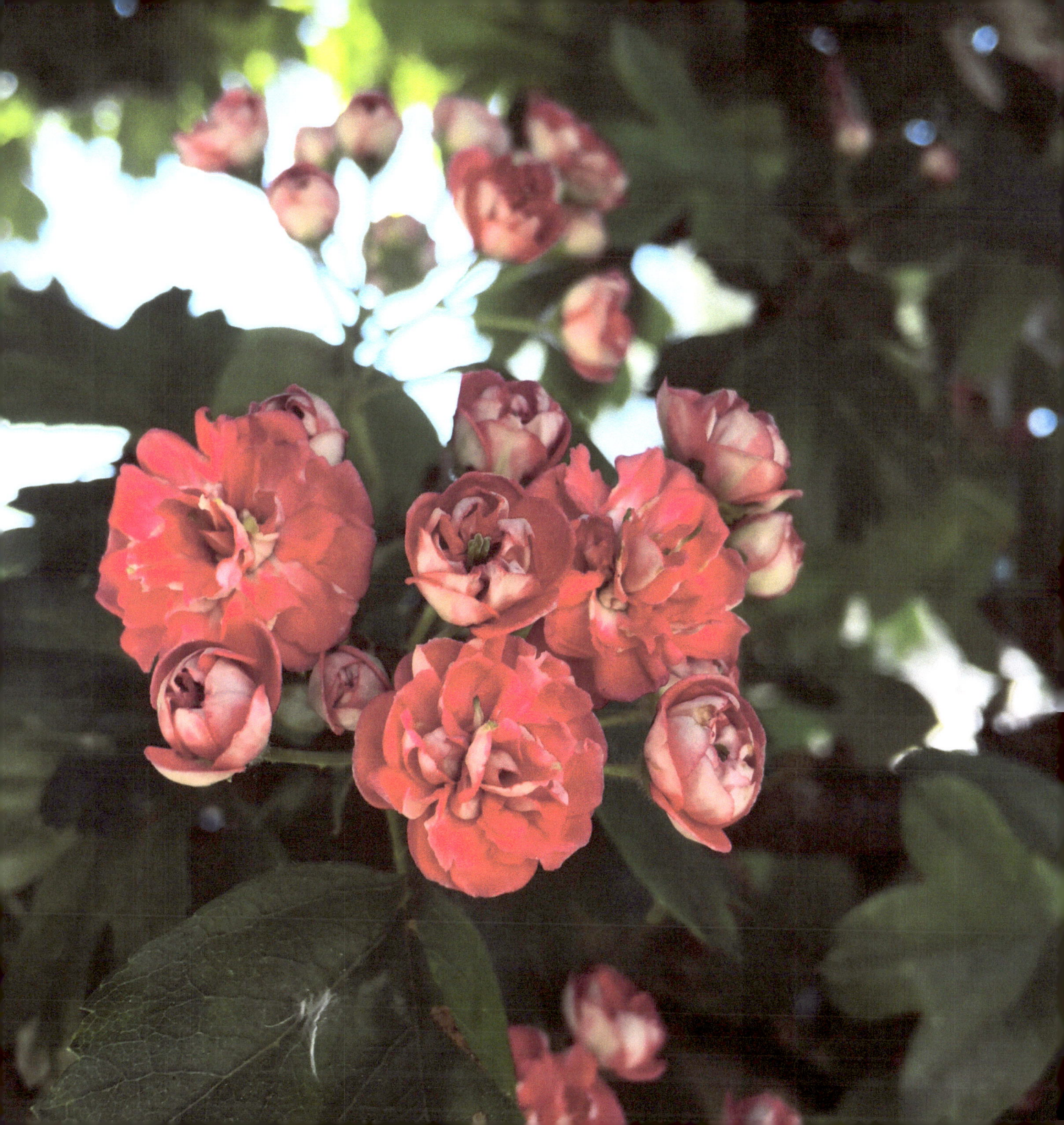

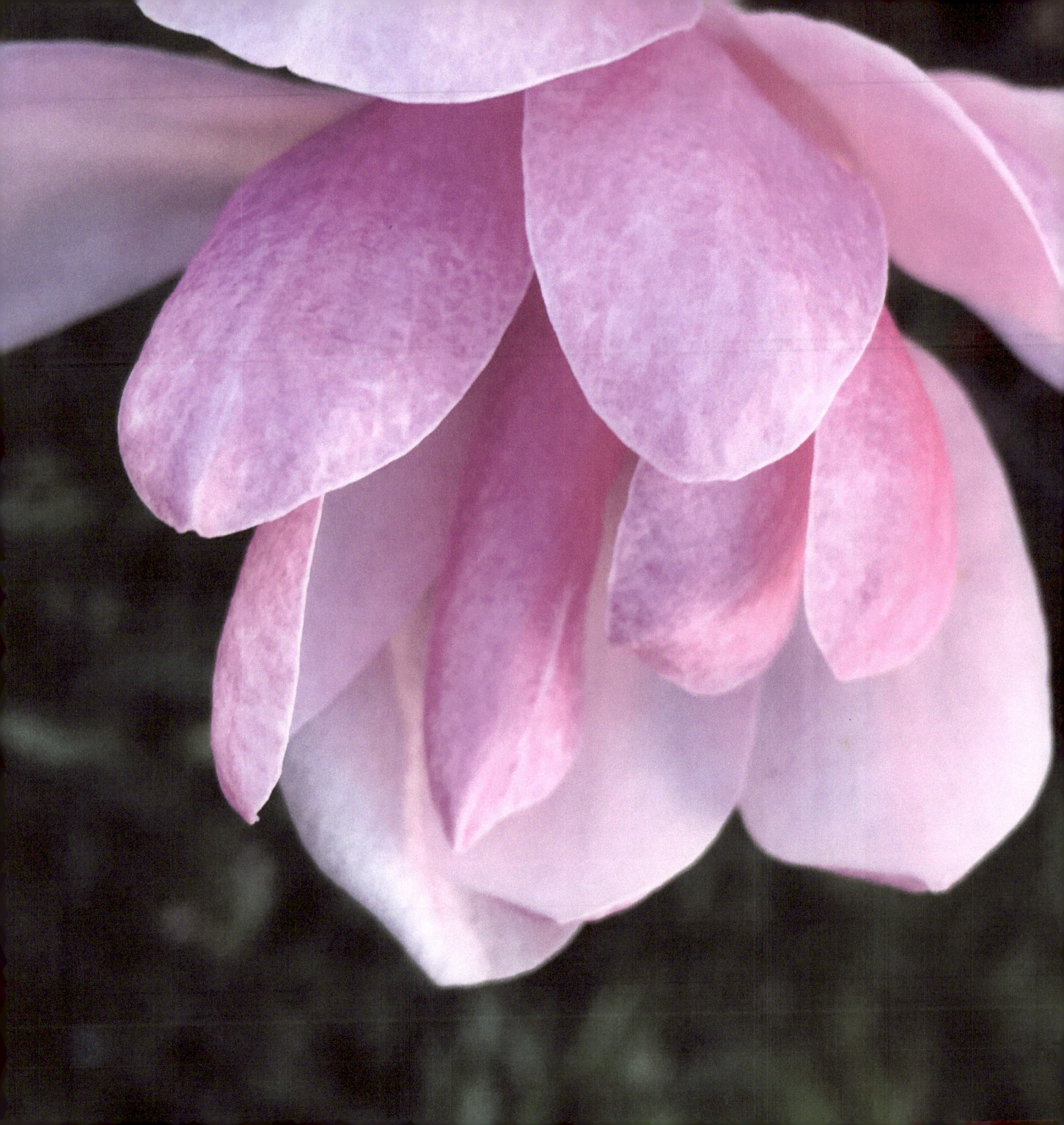

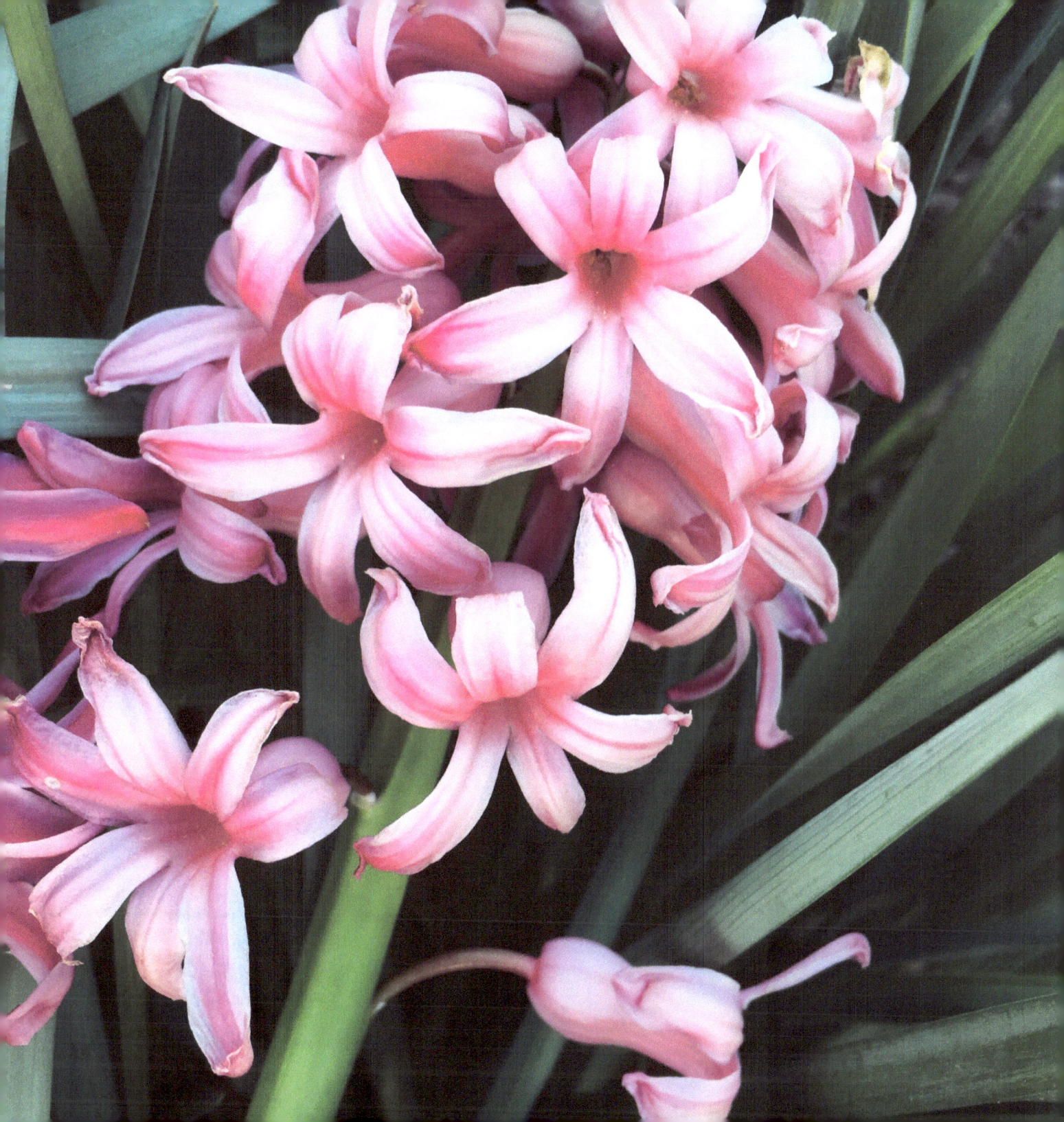

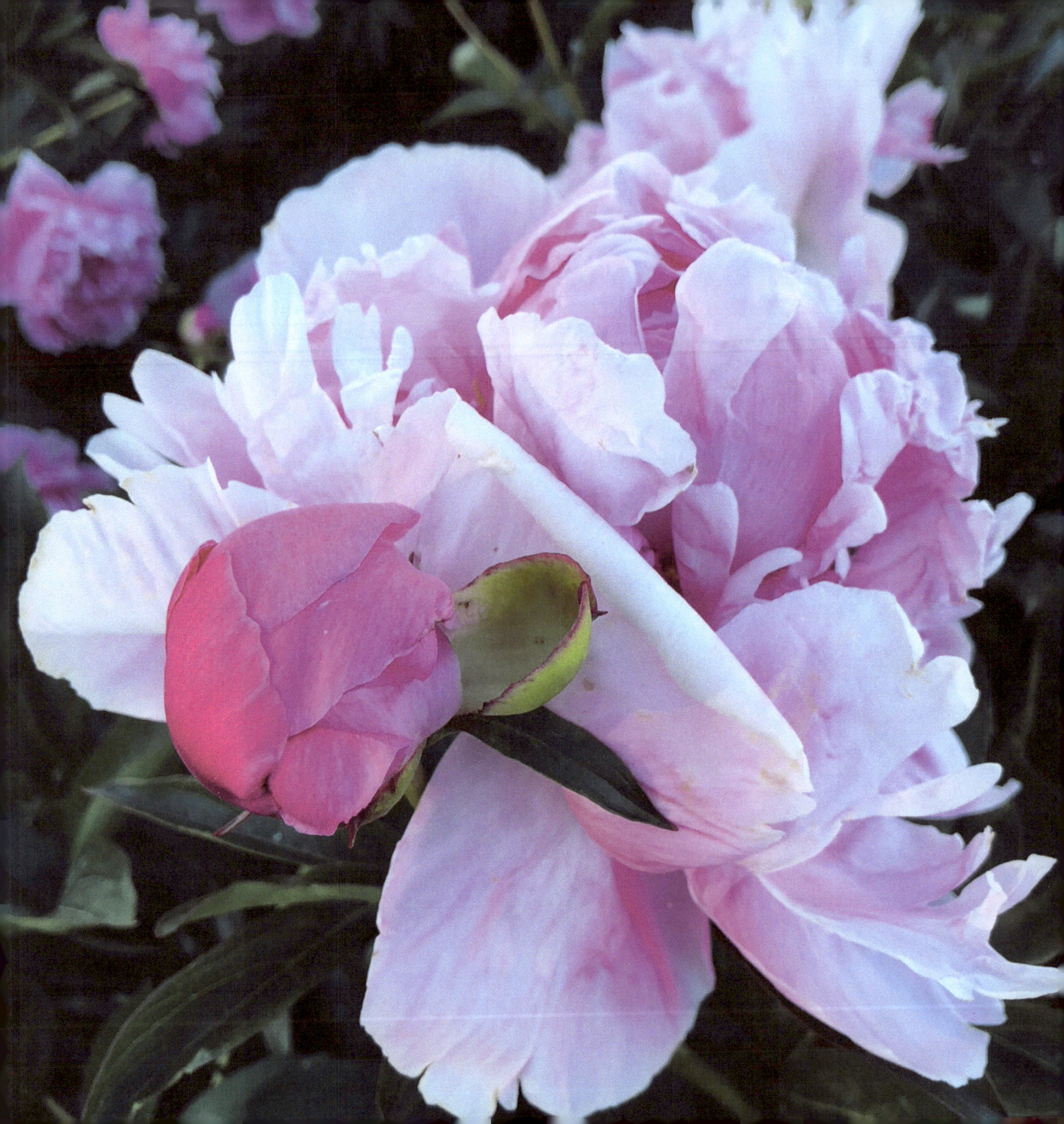

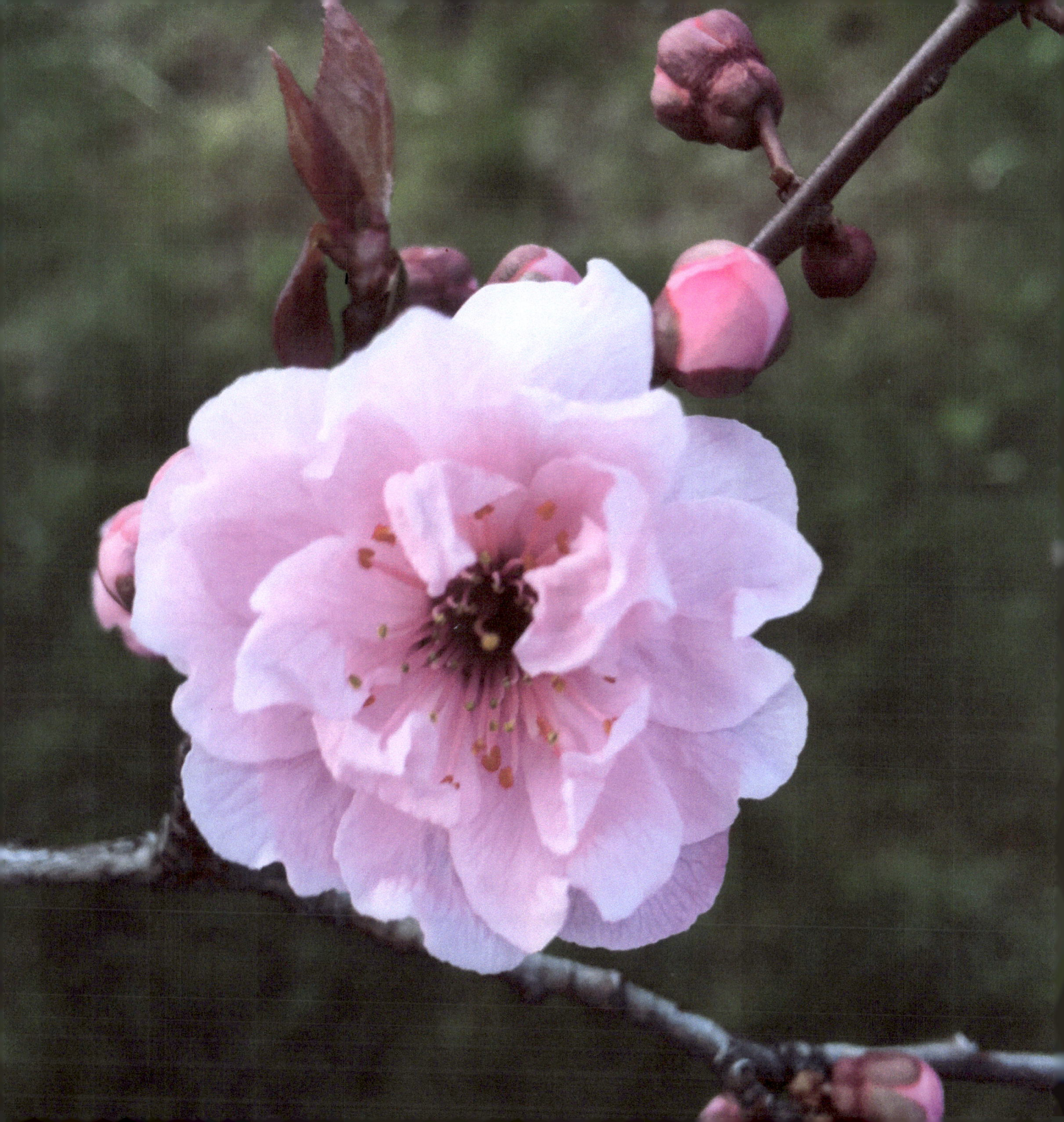

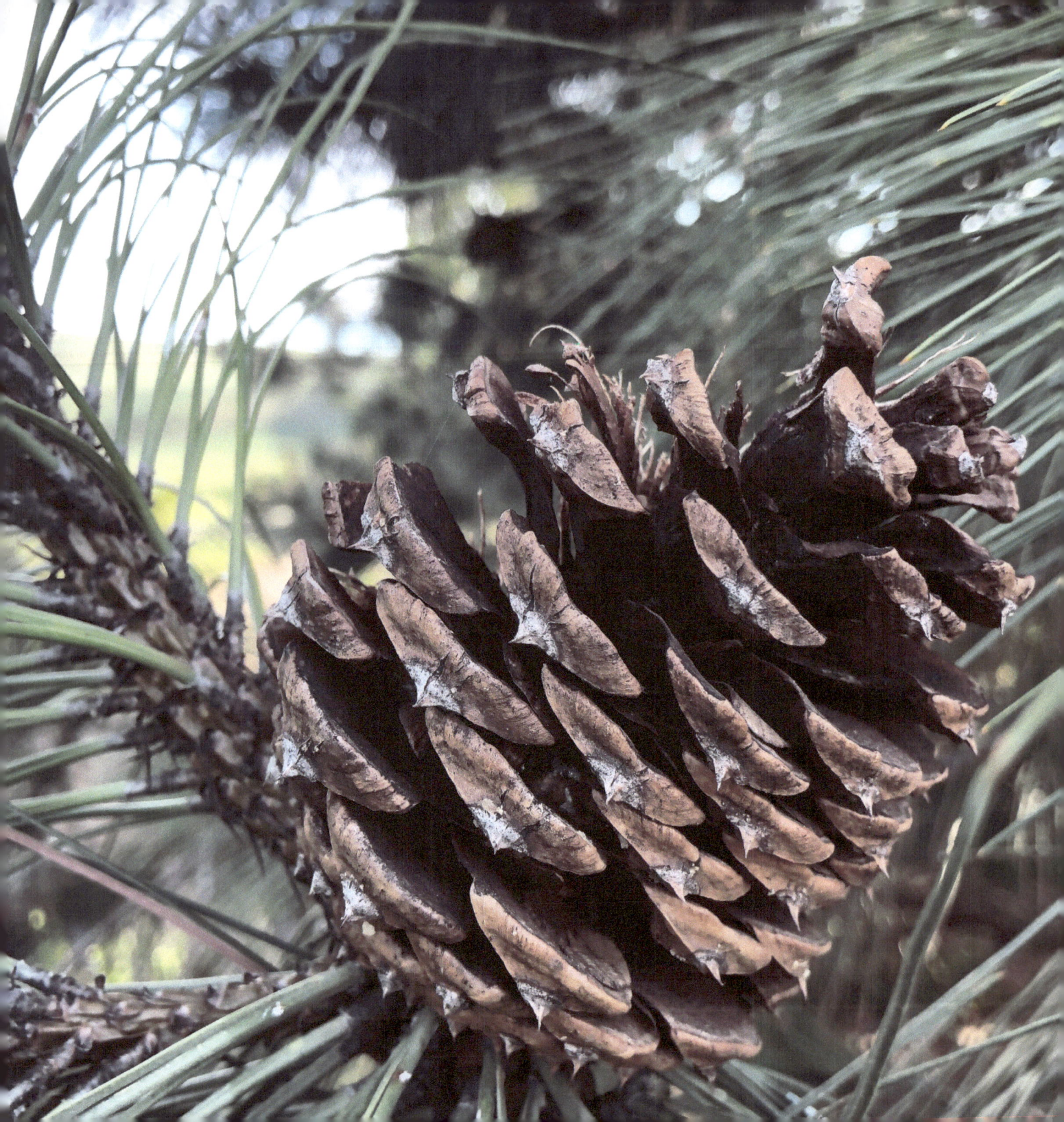

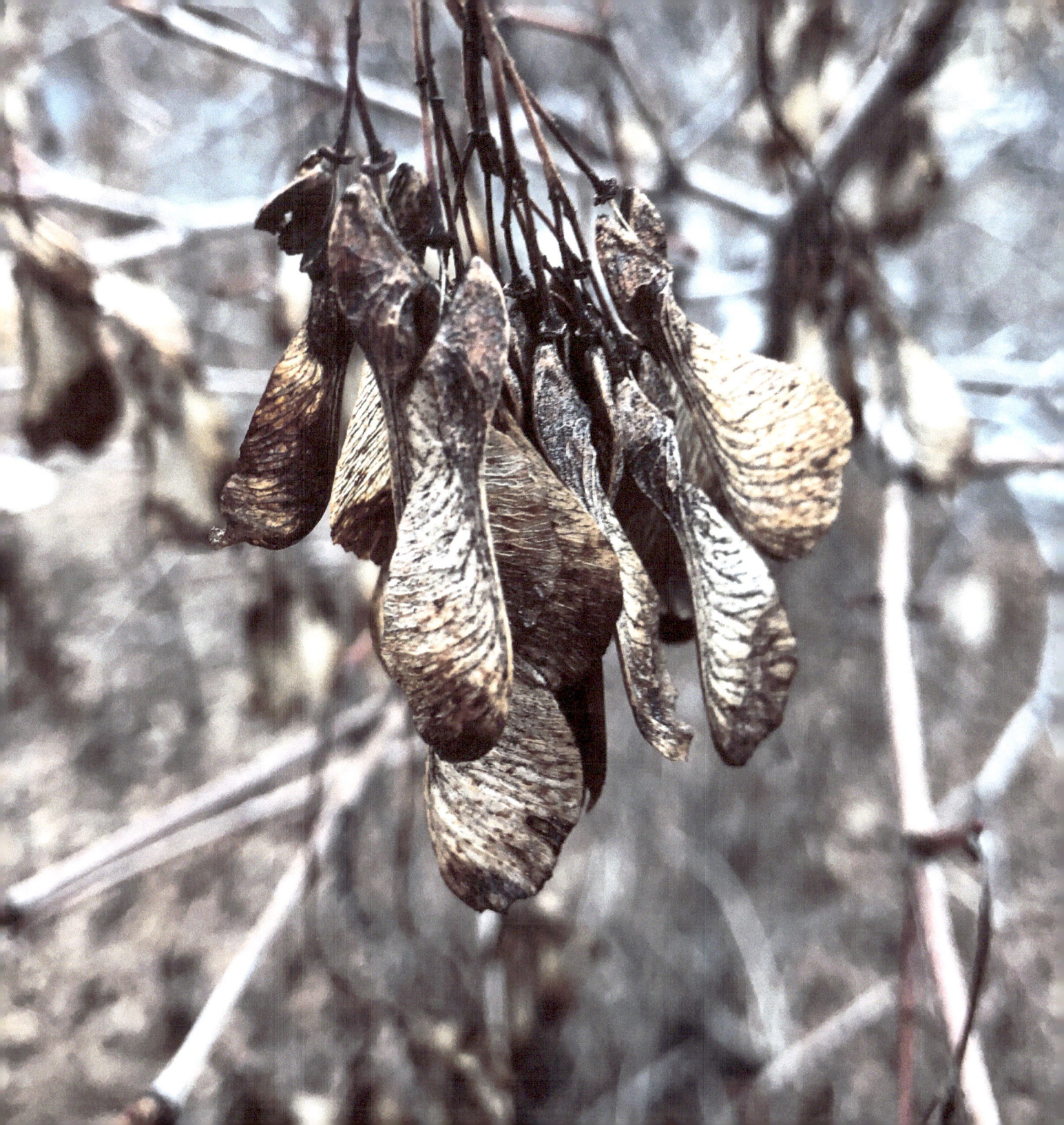

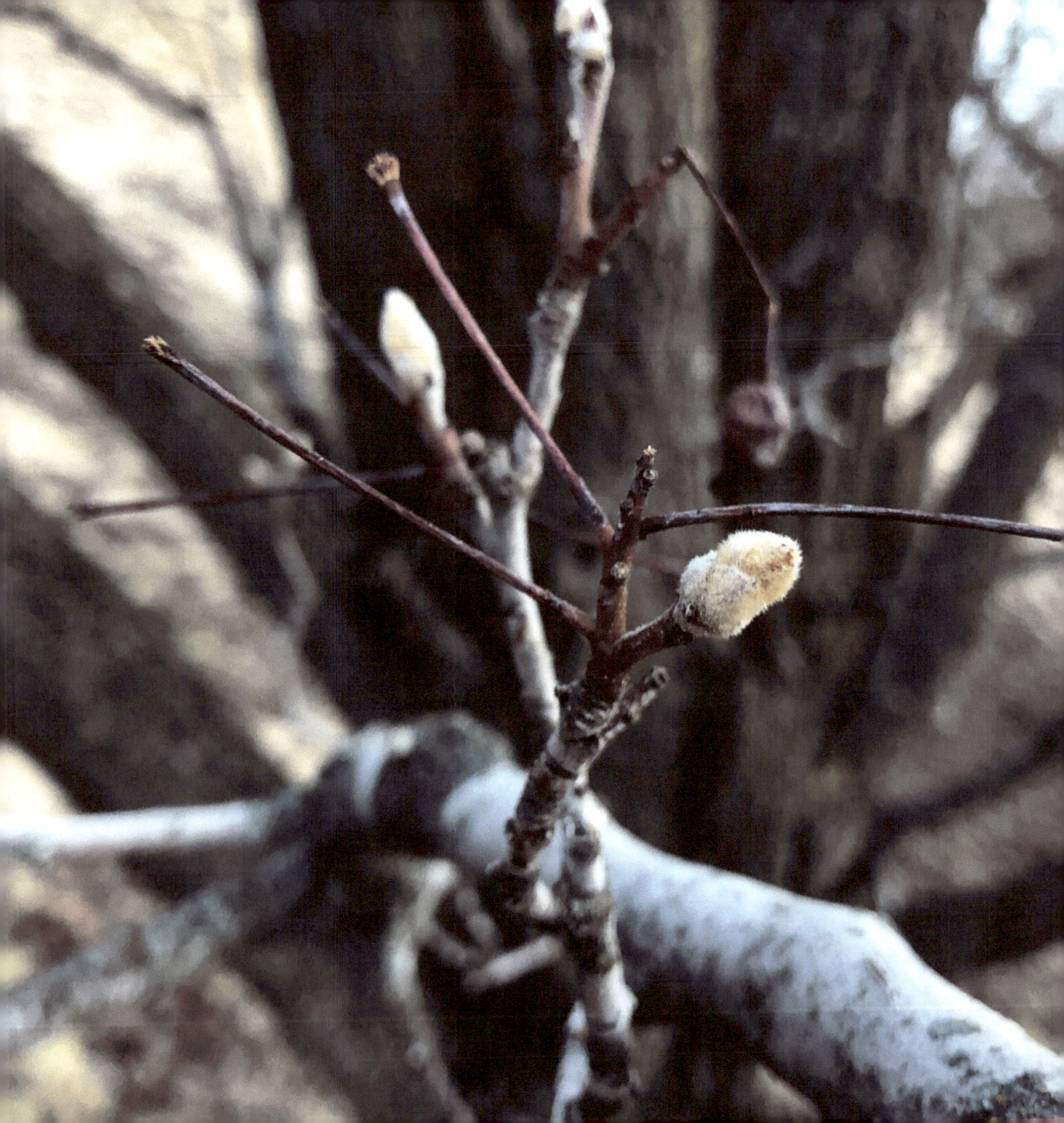

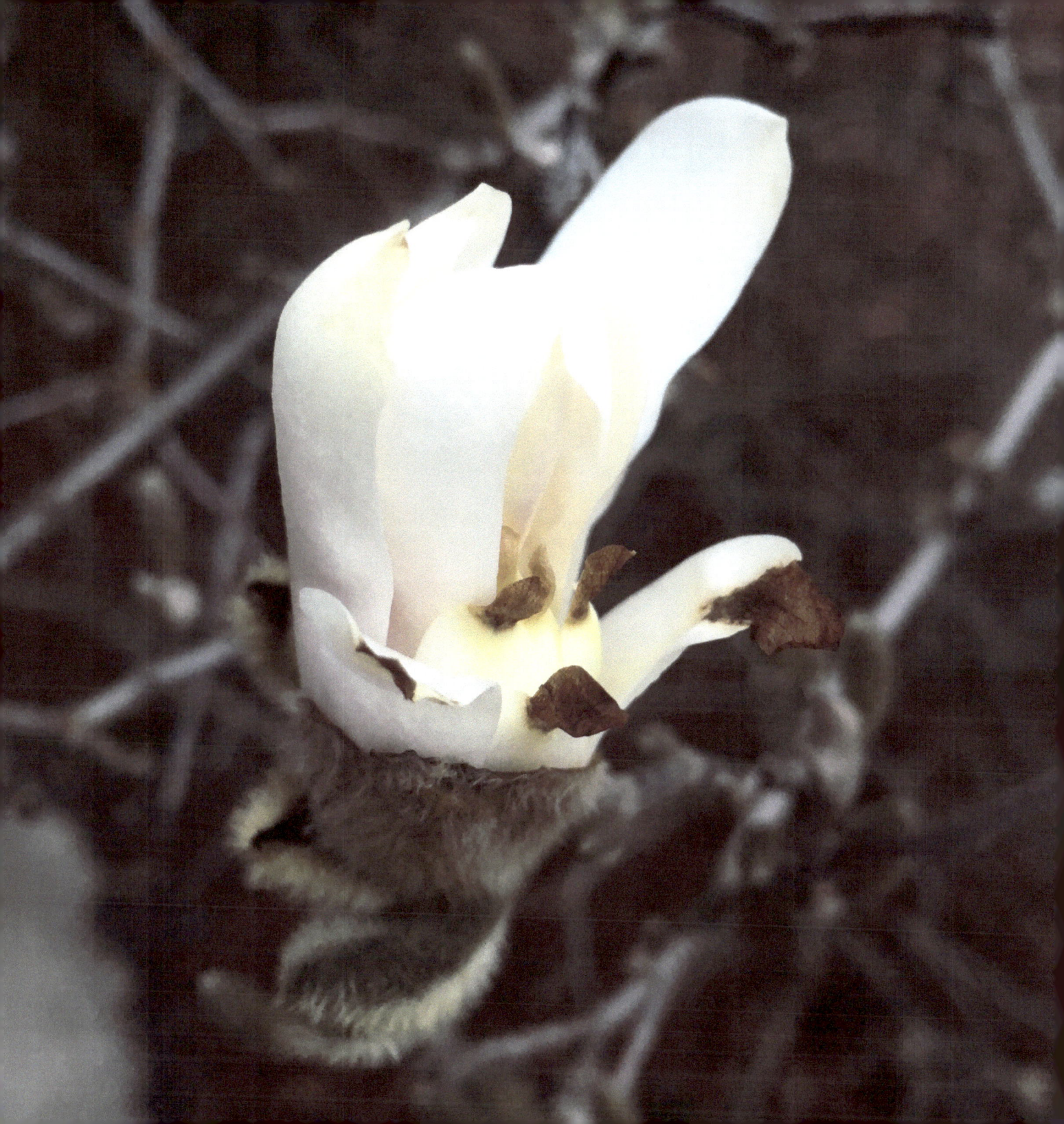

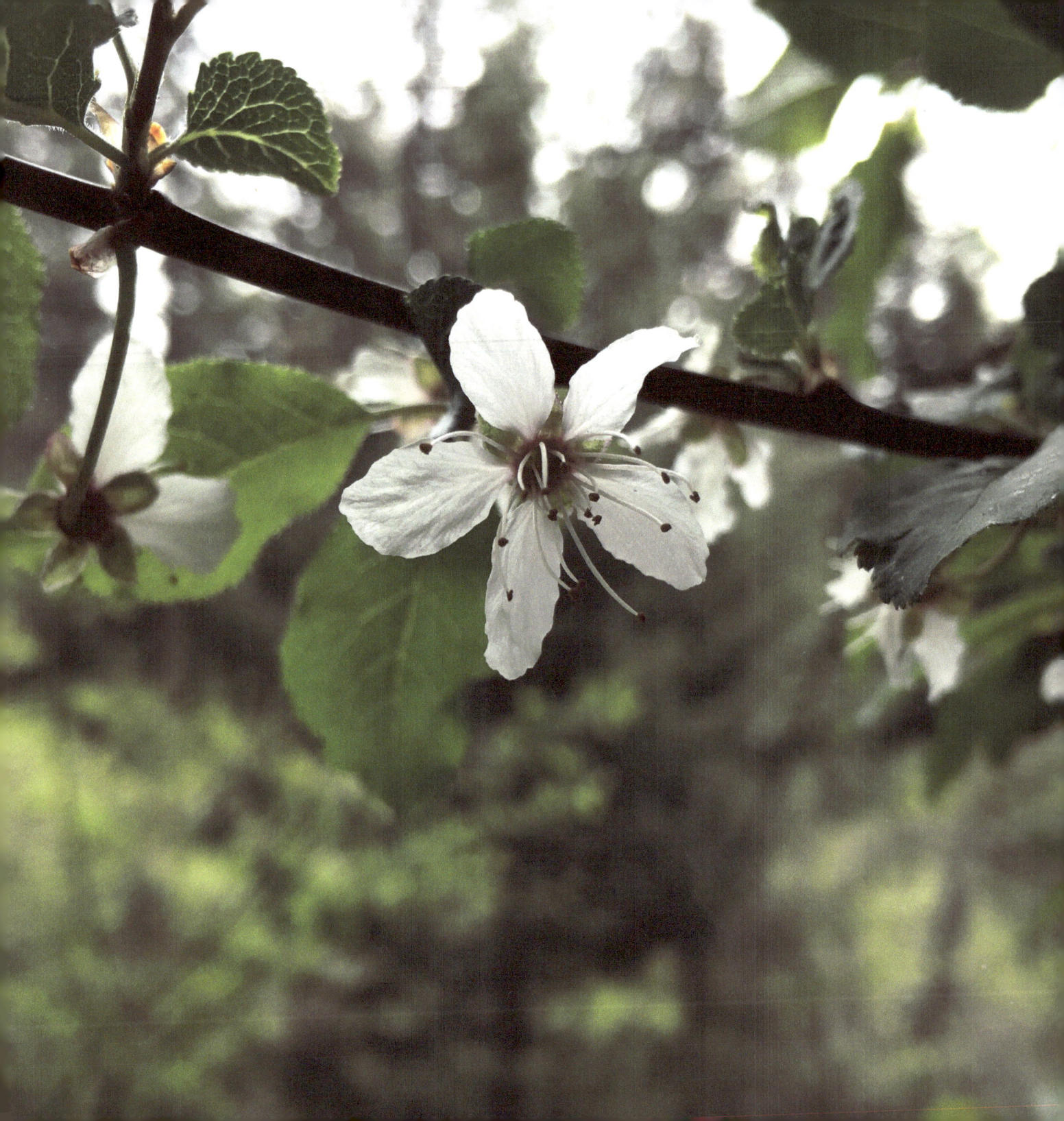

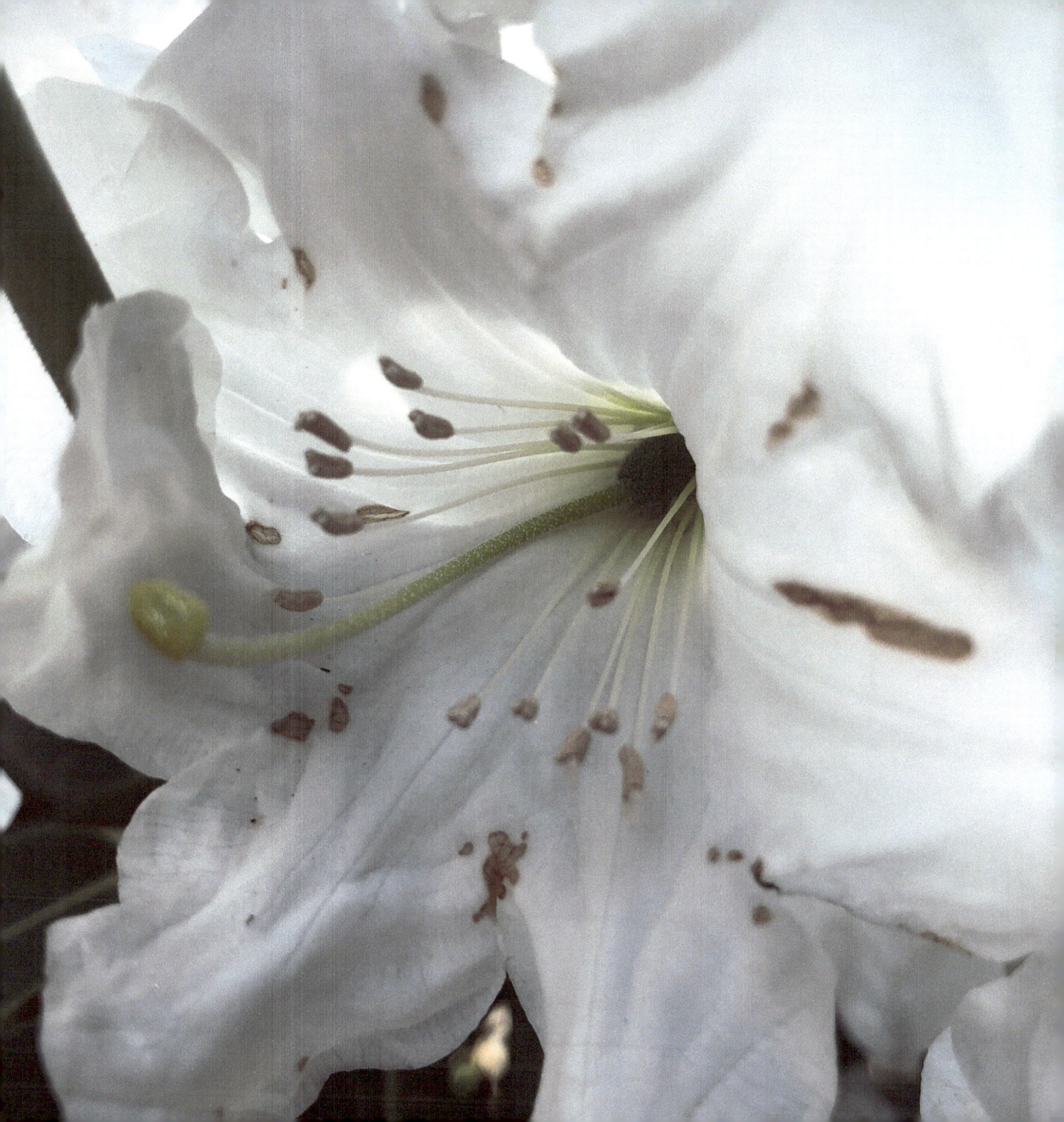

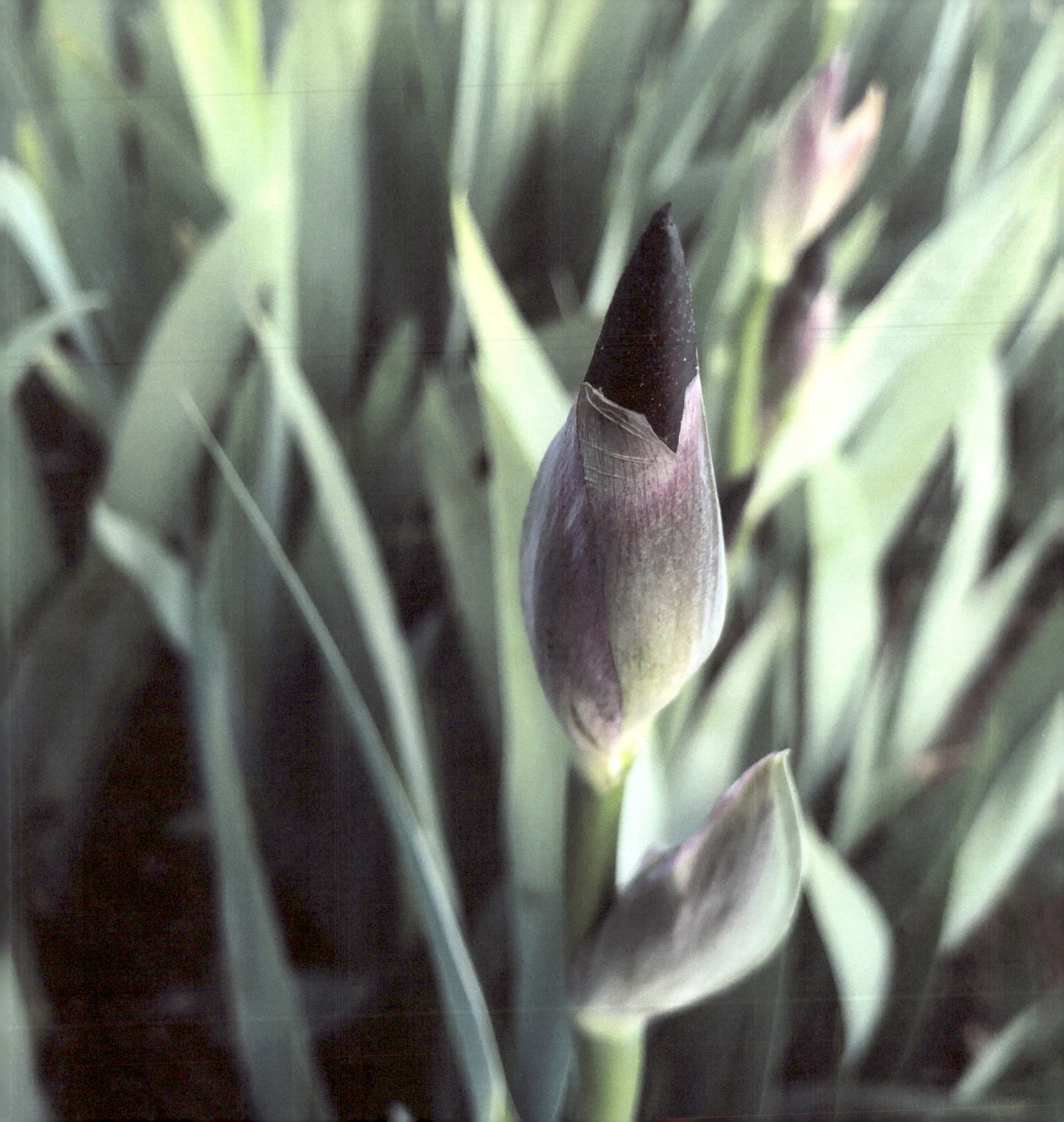

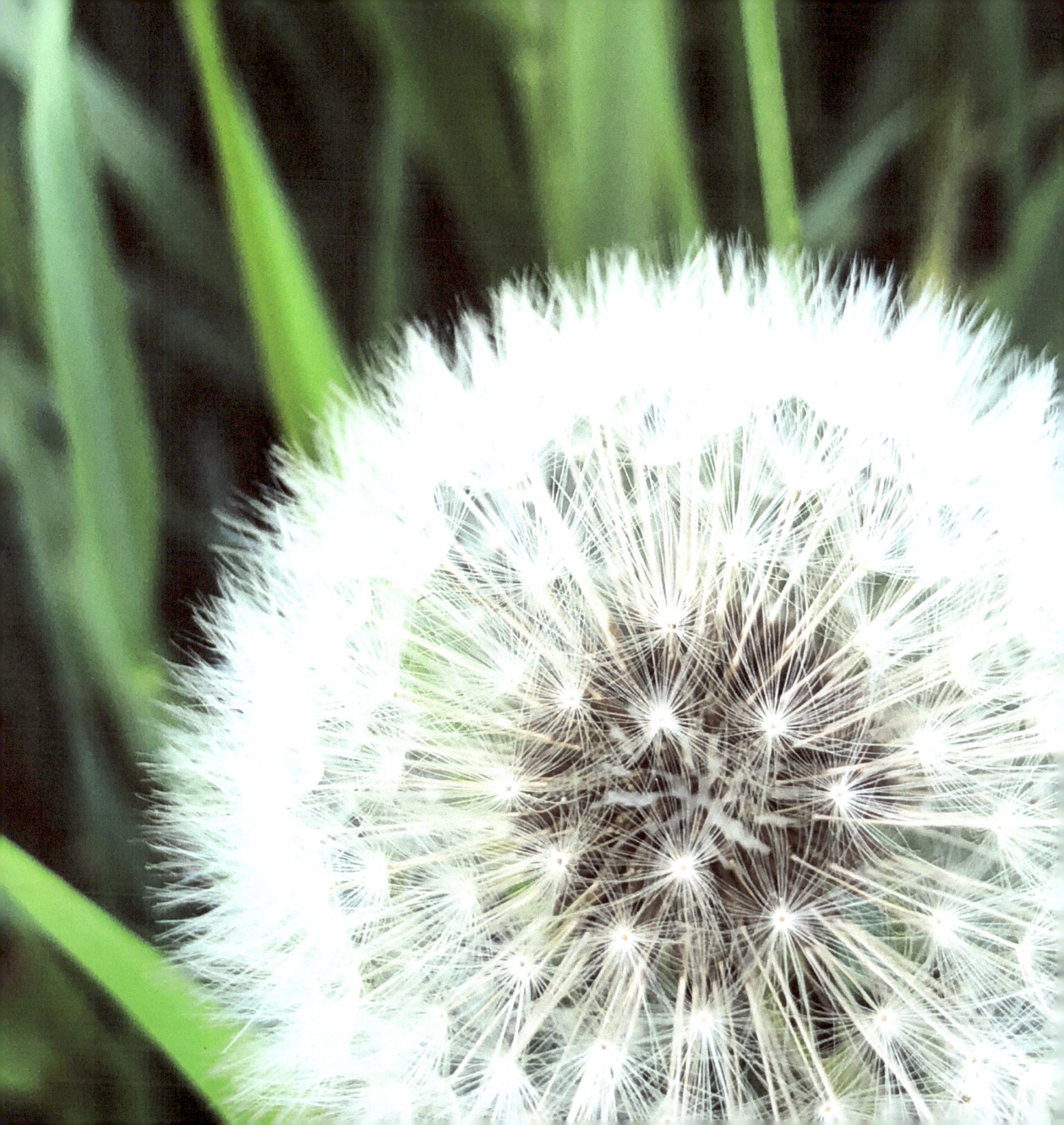

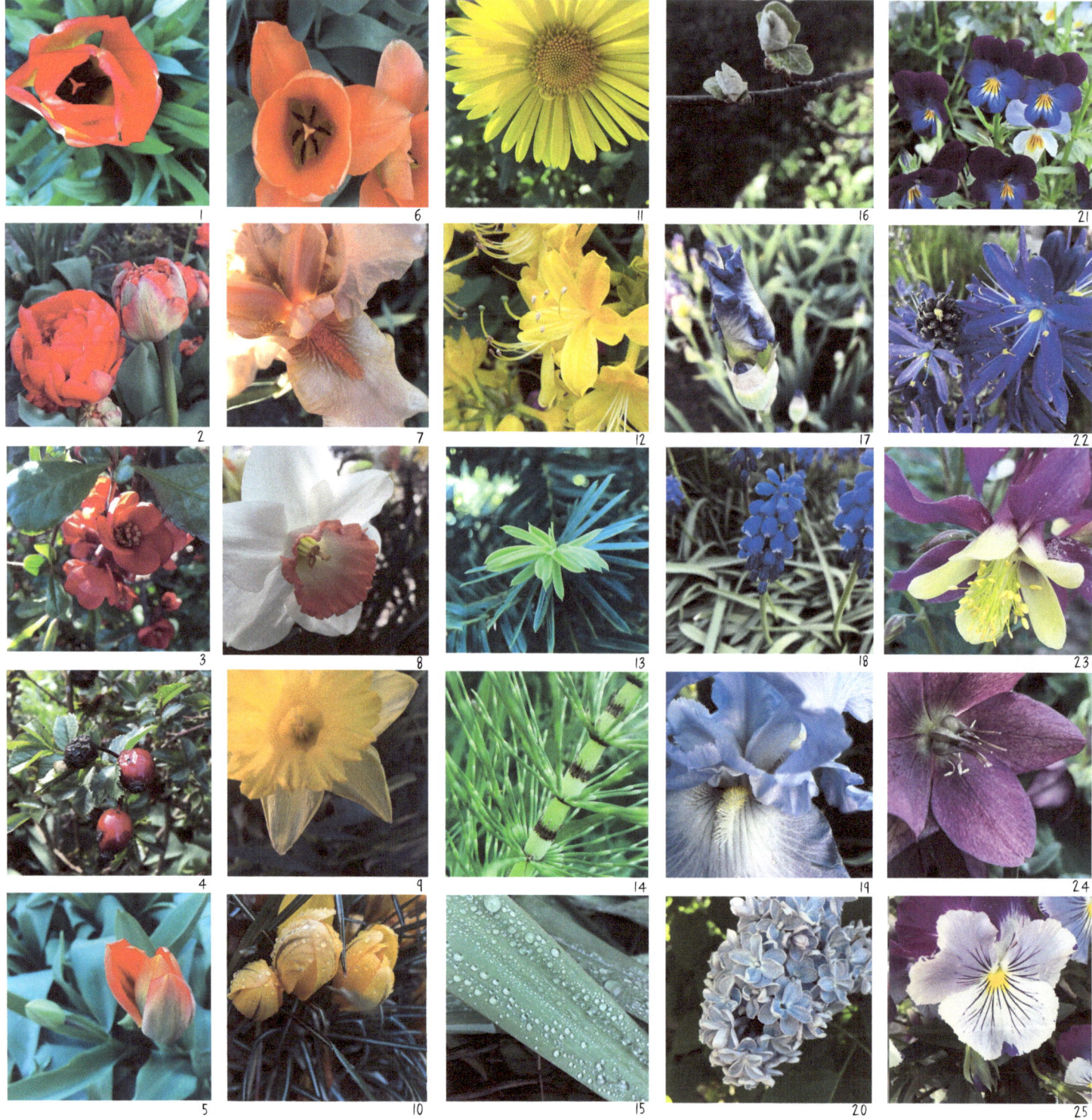

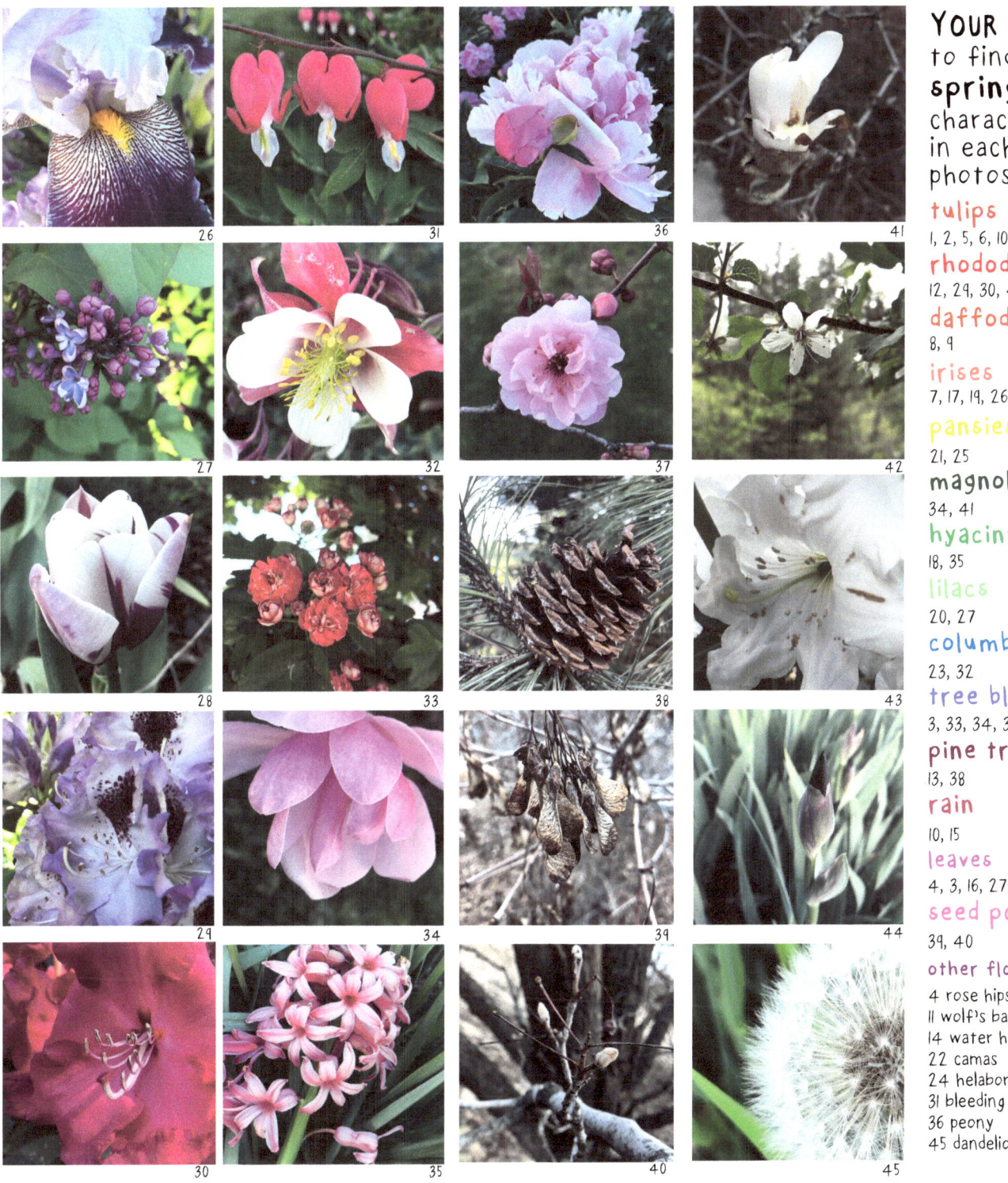

26 31 36 41
27 32 37 42
28 33 38 43
29 34 39 44
30 35 40 45

YOUR TURN
to find these
spring
characteristics
in each of the
photos:

tulips
1, 2, 5, 6, 10, 28
rhododendrons
12, 29, 30, 43
daffodils
8, 9
irises
7, 17, 19, 26, 44
pansies
21, 25
magnolias
34, 41
hyacinths
18, 35
lilacs
20, 27
columbines
23, 32
tree blossoms
3, 33, 34, 37, 41, 42
pine trees
13, 38
rain
10, 15
leaves
4, 3, 16, 27, 33, 42,
seed pods
39, 40
other flowers/plants
4 rose hips
11 wolf's bane
14 water horsetail
22 camas
24 helabora
31 bleeding heart
36 peony
45 dandelion

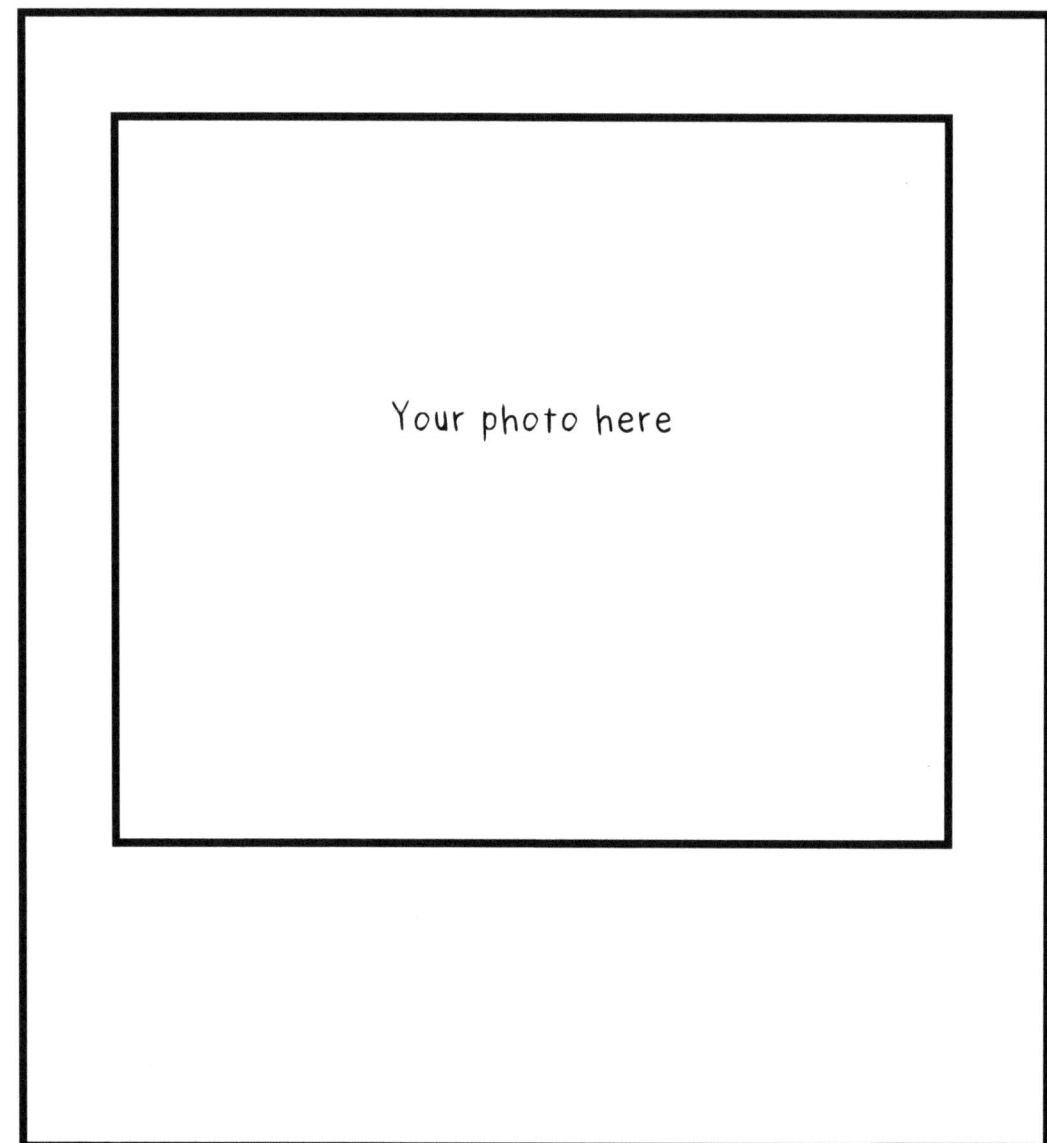

Your photo here

So now, YOU go & capture the **faces, characteristics** and **portraits** of nature that you see around you. I wish you well on your journey & may you start to see life in a new way.